1981

How to
Write & Sell
Magazine
Articles

Shirley Biagi

California State University, Sacramento

A SPECTRUM BOOK

Prentice-Hall, Inc., *Englewood Cliffs, N.J. 07632*

Library of Congress Cataloging in Publication Data

BIAGI, SHIRLEY
   How to write & sell magazine articles.

   (A Spectrum Book)
   Includes bibliographical references and index.
   1.-Authorship.   I.-Title.   II.-Title: How to write and
sell magazine articles.
PN147.B49   1981   808'.02   81-7316
                                       AACR2

ISBN 0-13-441618-X
ISBN 0-13-441600-7 {PBK.}

This Spectrum Book can be made available to businesses and organizations at a specal discount when ordered in large quantities. For more information, contact: Prentice-Hall, Inc., General Book Marketing, Special Sales Division, Englewood Cliffs, NJ 07632.

10 9 8 7 6 5 4 3 2 1

Printed in the United States of America

Editorial/production supervision and interior design by Donald Chanfrau
Cover design by Velthaus & King
Manufacturing buyer: Cathie Lenard

PRENTICE-HALL INTERNATIONAL, INC., London
PRENTICE-HALL OF AUSTRALIA PTY. LIMITED, Sydney
PRENTICE-HALL OF CANADA, LTD., Toronto
PRENTICE-HALL OF INDIA PRIVATE LIMITED, New Delhi
PRENTICE-HALL OF JAPAN, INC., Tokyo
PRENTICE-HALL OF SOUTHEAST ASIA PTE. LTD., Singapore
WHITEHALL BOOKS LIMITED, Wellington, New Zealand

For Vic, Paul, Tom, and David

Contents

7

RESEARCHING YOUR ARTICLE 60

8

HOW TO INTERVIEW 73

9

THE WRITER-PHOTOGRAPHER 87

10
WRITING YOUR FIRST DRAFT 100

11
THE LEGALITIES 110

12
THE FINAL DRAFT 130

Preface

When I first started writing, I was going to be the first writer who never received a rejection slip. I wrote this book with a little understanding, I hope, of the anxiety of a writer who reaches for a letter from the mailbox, wondering whether the answer is acceptance or rejection, or whether there is an answer at all.

After several rejections but also many acceptances, I offer what I have learned in ten years as a writer and as a teacher of magazine article writing. I give this book to all you nervous souls, standing by your mailboxes, but afraid to look inside.

© 1969 United Features Syndicate, Inc.

Acknowledgments

First, I must thank all my colleagues in the California State University, Sacramento, Journalism Department for their patient help. Special thanks to Ralph Talbert and Sharmon Goff for their advice on the photography chapter. For smoothing all the administrative bumps, I thank Betty Wolfman.

Gratitude to Lynn Ferry for her sensitive attention to detail in the photographs published in Chapter Nine. More gratitude to reference librarians Eugene Salmon, Cliff Wood, John Liberty, and Leah Freeman for coaxing me through card catalogs, pamphlet files, indexes, books, magazines and newspapers.

To my editor, Mary Kennan, I say thank you for believing I could do this, and most of all to Leigh Stephens I give continuous thanks for her unrelenting encouragement.

1

Understanding Magazines

SOME BACKGROUND

*I*n 1866, as the "Sandwich Islands Correspondent" for the *Sacramento Union*, Mark Twain agreed to a weekly fee of twenty dollars for each article he sent to the newspaper while on a voyage to Hawaii. The *Union* commissioned him for one letter a week, but like many free-lancers Twain needed money. So, in ten weeks he sent twenty-five articles. Today, his letters about the early Hawaiian settlements, *Mark Twain and Hawaii*, form an unmatched record of that territory.

Turn-of-the-century American muckraker Ida Tarbell, known for her exposure of the Standard Oil Company as a monopoly, began her writing career as a free-lancer, submitting articles purely on speculation to magazines in America while she paid her way through Europe. In Paris, American editor S. S. McClure ran up the eighty steps to Tarbell's apartment one day and knocked on her door. Her writing impressed him, he said, and would she write for his new magazine, *McClure's*, when she returned to the United States?

McClure's disheveled, disorganized manner made Tarbell doubt that he would ever start the magazine, yet she agreed to consider the idea. Tarbell grew even more doubtful about her future when, as McClure was leaving her apartment, he asked for a forty-dollar loan. She gave him the money, which she had been saving for a vacation.

Tarbell's doubts were misplaced, however, because for twenty-one years *McClure's* magazine was the very successful showcase for Tarbell, as well as for Lincoln Steffens and Rudyard Kipling. And McClure returned the forty dollars.

Editors are as diverse as their magazines. Writer Dorothy Parker claimed that *New Yorker* magazine editor Harold Ross had a "profound ignorance." He admitted he could not spell and once asked a colleague whether Moby Dick in the novel was the man or the whale. Yet, he attracted and published the writings of Dorothy Parker, Robert Benchley, James Thurber, Janet Flanner, and H. L. Mencken.

In *The Powers That Be*, author David Halberstam called *Time* founding editor Henry Luce "a curiously artless man, graceless and brusque and lonely, rude inevitably even to those whose favors and good will he coveted; he could only be what he was, he could never be facile or slick, though on frequent occasions his magazines were."[1]

Esquire founding editor Arnold Gingrich liked to wake at dawn to fish in the trout stream near his home. Then he dressed in natty tweeds for work, where he arrived early so he could practice his violin. *Esquire* published Hemingway, Fitzgerald, and Steinbeck under his direction.

American magazines will celebrate their 250th birthday in 1991. They have evolved from their polemical beginnings in 1741 with Ben Franklin's *General Magazine* and Andrew Bradford's *American Magazine* to the general interest magazines born in the

---

[1]David Halberstam, *The Powers That Be* (New York: Knopf, 1979).

1930s, such as *Life* and *Look,* to today's proliferation of specialized publications, such as *International Yachtsman* and *Dairy Goat Journal.*

THE MAGAZINE'S SUCCESS RATE

According to *Magazine Industry Market Place,* more than 350 magazines are created in the United States each year. Of these, only ten percent will survive the marketplace, which indicates the competitiveness of the magazine business. Competition among free-lancers for magazine space is equally vigorous, but the search by editors for writing talent continues.

Like Tarbell and Twain, some free-lancers want to become full-time magazine staff writers. Some writers earn a majority of their income from free-lancing. But most free-lancers, including those who work as professional journalists, look to free-lancing as a hobby, a way to make some extra money, and an interesting sideline to satisfy their curiosity.

COMPANY, TRADE, AND CONSUMER MAGAZINES

The term "free lance" originally meant a medieval mercenary soldier with a lance for hire. Today's free-lancer must be equally versatile.

More than 5,000 magazines in the United States publish free-lance articles. These magazines can be divided into three categories—company publications, trade publications, and consumer publications.

Company publications are produced by a specific company or industry mainly for its employees, stockholders, and customers. Trade publications are produced by businesses for professional retailers, manufacturers, and technical experts in a particular industry. Consumer publications are all those popularly marketed at newsstands, in supermarkets, and bookstores.

Employees of the Underwood Company, for example, may read *The Red Devil*, a company publication that emphasizes food products and the history of food, while your grocer reads the trade publication *Progressive Grocer* to learn how to create a more attractive canned meat display and you read the consumer publication *Family Circle* to learn how to use minced ham to stretch your food budget. All these are free-lance markets, yet clearly each has a different audience, which in turn dictates the magazine's content.

HOW MAGAZINES ARE ORGANIZED

Magazines, small and large, follow a predictable pattern of organization. The larger the magazine, the more elaborate the staff.

Overseeing both the business and the writing on a magazine is the publisher, who owns the publication. The publisher may sometimes also be the editor, but more often these functions are separate.

The business side must organize subscriptions, advertising, marketing, and production of the magazine. The editorial side worries about what goes inside the magazine and how the magazine looks.

Most magazines, except for those concerned with personalities *(People)* and news *(Time* and *Newsweek)*, have a three-to-four-month lead time from final copy to publication. So, editors celebrate Christmas in August or September and get ready for the Fourth of July in the winter.

Magazine editors use charts to track future magazines and their status in production. An editor of a monthly magazine may have three issues going at once, so each of these issues is assigned to an associate editor.

A magazine's size each month is decided by the size of the issue at the same time the year before and the number of advertisements sold for each issue. A consumer magazine usually runs about forty percent ads and sixty percent copy. A magazine may also produce regional editions, which means that articles from separate portions of the country must be coordinated with advertising, and sometimes even articles, specifically for a regional audience.

Many magazines employ staff writers to produce regular features on specific subjects, such as gardening or cooking. These staff-written features can be set in type ahead of time, which helps speed production. A magazine may also accumulate a backlog of free-lance articles once scheduled to run in previous issues from which the editor can draw last-minute fillers.

REVIEWING FREE-LANCE IDEAS

At a large magazine, free-lance article ideas must survive several levels of review before even reaching the editor for approval. Often editorial assistants sort most of the incoming mail, sending form rejection slips for poorly conceived or inappropriate articles and passing promising ideas to the next level of review, usually an assistant or associate editor.

The assistant or associate editor sends letters to people whose ideas show potential and may either write a personal note of rejection for unappealing ideas or return this responsibility to an editorial assistant.

Sometimes associate editors need approval from the editor to send a writer a go-ahead, and some magazines use an editorial review board of several people to make these decisions.

At small magazines, of course, the editor may be the only one to review and approve an article because there are no filtering levels. At a very small magazine, in fact, the editor may not only read the mail directly, but may also open the mail, answer the telephone, and handle the office with occasional part-time help.

An editor who assigns an article to a free-lancer may tentatively schedule the article for a specific issue. If the free-lancer is new to the magazine, however, the editor waits until the copy is in and accepted before setting a date. The art editor meanwhile coordinates photographs, cartoons, and/or graphics.

Where articles will appear in the magazine is decided early in the editorial process, although changes can be made if current events make a particular article topical. An article that appears before the middle fold in the magazine is traditionally considered more prominent than an article near the end.

HOW A MAGAZINE IS PRINTED

An editor can choose one of three ways to print the magazine—letterpress, offset, or photogravure. Most magazines use letterpress and offset because photogravure is very time-consuming.

Letterpress uses metal type set in frames, which are then inked and set on paper. *Cosmopolitan, Time,* and *Family Circle* use letterpress.

Offset uses photography to take pictures of what is to be printed. Many newspapers, as well as *Newsweek* and *House Beautiful,* use this quick process because changes are easy and inexpensive.

For photogravure, acid etches impressions in a copper cylinder, which rotates in ink and prints on paper under pressure. This provides better shadings of color, but requires more preparation time than either letterpress or offset. *TV Guide* and *Reader's Digest* use photogravure.

So, for each issue covers must be designed, articles must be organized, artwork must be approved, styles and sizes of type must be set, and deadlines must be met. Into all of this must fit the free-lancer.

FOR MORE INFORMATION

For more details concerning magazine publishing, read *The Magazine* by Leonard Mogel of the *National Lampoon* (Prentice-Hall, 1979).

Also, Harvard University Press publishes a five-volume history of American magazines, 1741–1930, by Frank L. Mott, appropriately titled *A History of American Magazines.*

Folio: The Magazine for Magazine Management is the publication of the magazine industry, published monthly from New Canaan, Connecticut. *Folio* also publishes *Handbook of Magazine Publishing*, a collection of more than 160 articles taken from *Folio* on the fundamentals of publishing a magazine successfully.

2

Learning
Which Ideas Sell

To know what to write, you must first know what sells. This sounds too simple, but the most common mistake beginning free-lancers make is that they decide what to write without understanding the market.

Remember—you are not a fiction writer, stashed in a closet for a year with your novel, refusing all food, threatening suicide, raving about how you will never truly be able to unravel your characters' personalities, never considering whether anyone will want to buy what you write.

Record your fantasies and your self-analysis in your daily journal and save them for the novel you may someday write. Successful nonfiction magazine free-lancers base their articles on reality, not imagination, and their ideas must be both tangible and marketable.

SOURCES FOR MAGAZINE WRITING

The first source you should check to learn what magazines want is the current edition of *Writer's Market*, an annually updated, comprehensive collection of company, trade, and consumer magazines that buy free-lance material. Your library will have a copy, although you probably will want to buy the book, since *Writer's Market* (published by Writer's Digest Books, Cincinnati, Ohio) is as indispensable to the free-lancer as a dictionary.

Writer's Market lists each magazine's address and usually the name of the editor. Also included are magazine circulation, type of articles each magazine seeks, whether the magazine accepts photographs, and how much the magazine pays. You can check whether the magazine is copyrighted and whether you must query the editor (write a letter about your article) before submitting a manuscript.

COSMOPOLITAN, 224 W. 57th St., New York NY 10019. Editor: Helen Gurley Brown. Managing Editor: Guy Flatley. For career women, ages 18 to 34. Monthly. Circ. 2,500,000. Buys all rights. Pays on acceptance. Not interested in receiving unsolicited manuscripts. Most material is assigned to established, known professional writers who sell regularly to top national markets, or is commissioned through literary agents.

Nonfiction and Photos: Not interested in unsolicited manuscripts; for agents and top professional writers, requirements are as follows: "We want pieces that tell an attractive, 18 to 34-year-old, intelligent, good-citizen girl how to have a more rewarding life—'how-to' pieces, 'self-improvement pieces,' as well as articles which deal with more serious matters. We'd be interested in articles on careers, part-time jobs, diets, food, fashion, men, the entertainment world, emotions, money, medicine and psychology, and fabulous characters." Uses some first person stories. Logical, interesting, authoritave writing is a must, as is a feminist consciousness. Length: 1,200-1,500 words; 3,000-4,000 words. Pays $200-500 for short pieces, $1,000-1,750 for longer articles. Photos purchased on assignment only.

Fiction: Department Editor: Harris Dienstfrey. Not interested in unsolicited manuscripts; for agents and top professional writers, requirements are as follows: "Good plotting and excellent writing are important. We want short stories dealing with adult subject matter which would interest a sophisticated audience, primarily female, 18-34. We prefer serious quality fiction or light tongue-in-cheek stories on any subject, done in good taste. We love stories dealing with contemporary man-woman relationships. Short-shorts are okay but we prefer them to have snap or 'trick' endings. The formula story, the soap opera, skimpy mood pieces or character sketches are not for us." Length: short-shorts, 1,500-3,000 words; short stories, 4,000-6,000 words; condensed novels and novel excerpts. "We also use murder or suspense stories of about 25,000-30,000 words dealing with the upper class stratum of American living. A foreign background is acceptable, but the chief characters should be American." Has published the work of Agatha Christie, Joyce Carol Oates, Evan Hunter, and other established writers. Pays about $1,000 and up for short stories and novel excerpts, $4,500 and up for condensed novels.[1]

Central to each description in *Writer's Market* is the type of article the magazine editor likes to see. One editor may prefer "informational, interview, profile, historical, think articles and book reviews," while another looks for articles about "social and civic betterment, business, education, religion, domestic affairs."

Do not be discouraged if a magazine such as *Cosmopolitan* says it does not accept unsolicited manuscripts. Instead, you will write a letter (called a query letter) describing your article.

Like all professions, magazine writing has its shorthand, so some of the abbreviations and terminology in *Writer's Market* may be unfamiliar to the beginner. Examples are shown below.

All rights. See Chapter Eleven.

B & W. Black-and-white photograph.

First North American Serial Rights. See Chapter Eleven.

Kill fee. A fee paid by a magazine to a writer when a contracted article is not used.

---

[1]Reprinted courtesy *Writer's Market*, F&W Publishing Co., 9933 Alliance Rd., Cincinnati, Ohio 45242. All rights reserved. © Copyright 1980.

Ms. Abbreviation for manuscript.

Mss. More than one manuscript.

Multiple queries. Simultaneously sending several letters to different magazines describing the same article idea. See Chapter Four.

Multiple submissions. Sending completed articles simultaneously to several magazines. See Chapter Four.

One-time rights. See Chapter Eleven.

Payment on acceptance. As soon as the editor decides to use your article, your check is sent.

Payment on publication. You must wait until the magazine uses your article to be paid.

Query. A letter you send to the editor describing your article idea.)

Reprint rights. See Chapter Eleven.

SASE. Self-addressed, stamped envelope.

Speculation. The editor will read your material, but makes no guarantee about buying it.

Writer's Market is the traditional free-lance marketing source, but it by no means provides all the information or all the magazines that are possible markets for your ideas. To understand markets thoroughly you should also know about several other publications that detail magazine and newspaper statistics. These overlapping, but very helpful resources on magazine markets are listed below.

Ayer's Directory of Newspapers, Magazines and Trade Publications contains specialized sections on religious, black, college, trade, and fraternal publications.

The International Directory of Little Magazines and Small Presses is exactly what it says. Many of these are not paying markets, but several quality publications are listed.

Magazine Industry Market Place, first published in 1980, calls itself "The Directory of American Periodical Publishing." For the magazines listed, MIMP includes the magazine's address and phone number, major editors, how often the magazine is published, subscription prices, advertising rates, and a one-sentence audience description.

Cosmopolitan[2]
Hearst Corp
224 W 57 St, New York 10019
    Tel: 212-262-5700
Subn Address: Box 10074, Des Moines, IA 50340
Publisher: Louis E Porterfield
Ed: Helen Gurley Brown
Man Ed: Guy Flatley
Book Review Eds: Harris Dienstfrey, Alison Cooper
Prodn Mgrs: Thomas Sedita, Jane Fleming
Art Dir: Linda Cox
Adv Dir: William T Hunt
Br Off: 1 N Wacker Dr, Chicago, IL 60606
    Tel: 312-984-5111
    Adv Mgr: Robert A Rose
Circ: 2,747,042 paid, 8386 cont; ABC audit Dec 1979
Printer: World Color Press
Frequency: Monthly
344 pp: $1.50/issue, $21/yr
Advertising: b&w & color, b&w page $17,580, trim 8 x 10⅞, prints demographic editions
Adv Sales Rep: Perkins, Stephen, von der Lieth & Hayward
Member: MPA
Edited for young women interested in self-improvement with articles on careers, clothes, beauty, travel, entertainment & the arts.
First published: 1896
ISSN: 0010-9541

MIMP also separately lists advertising agencies, market researchers, associations, newsletters, and reference books about maga-

[2]Reprinted from *Magazine Industry Market Place* with permission of the R. R. Bowker Company. Copyright © 1980 by Xerox Corporation.

zine publishing. MIMP is an expansion of the magazine section in *Literary Market Place*, the "business directory to American book publishing." LMP still contains a magazine section, but it also lists book clubs, book publishers, syndicates, literary prizes, and awards.

Magazines for Libraries gives detailed information about each magazine's audience, but its updating is not as current as the other marketing guides.

Standard Rate and Data Survey is a monthly (and, as a result, very current) directory of advertising rates, circulation information, and descriptions of formats published in separate volumes for magazines, newspapers, and business publications.

Working Press of the Nation is a directory of people employed in all aspects of publishing and the media, published annually in five volumes—Newspapers (Volume I), Magazines (Volume II), Radio/TV (Volume III), Free-lancers (Volume IV), and House Magazines (Volume V). Volumes I, II, and V will be the most helpful. Listed are editors, readership, size, and format of each publication. Volumes III and IV are good resources for broadcasting and writing contacts.

HOW TO DO A MARKETING ANALYSIS

To do a marketing analysis, you compare what the marketing directories say about magazines with the actual magazine. Copy the marketing information for at least five magazines to which you would like to contribute from the current edition of at least two of these marketing resources (such as *Writer's Market* and *Magazine Industry Market Place*). Then answer these questions:

1. How often is the magazine published?
2. What is the magazine's circulation?
3. What types of articles does each magazine use?

4. Must a writer query before sending an article?
5. Is the magazine copyrighted?
6. Does the magazine accept photographs?
7. How much does the magazine pay?
8. What is the preferred article length?

Next, examine two recent copies of each magazine to become more familiar with the publication and to augment your knowledge about the market. Then answer these questions:

1. Is the publication slick (shiny) or is it printed on newsprint or other types of paper? A slick publication usually devotes considerable money to production. A review of the artwork and whether the magazine uses color throughout will help you intuit whether the magazine is an expensive product.

2. Is the magazine published as frequently as the market listing shows? A magazine that is publishing less frequently may be having money problems, which indicates a market to avoid until the publication stabilizes. A magazine that is publishing more frequently indicates a better market for your articles, since more material will be needed.

3. Does the editor's name on the masthead in the current issue match the market listing? The magazine business is very fluid, and, of course, you will want to query the current editor.

4. Read the Editor's Note, which appears in the front of most magazines. Often this will reveal topics planned for upcoming issues, so you can avoid duplicating an idea.

5. Check the contents. What kinds of articles does the magazine seem to be running regularly? Are there staff-written sections? Staff writers usually are identified in the masthead (the listing near the front, of people who work for the magazine) or by a "Staff Writer" title under their by-line (name as author of an article). If staff writers are producing regular features on camera repair or mealtime tips, for example, you should market your ideas on these topics to another magazine. Subtract the total number of articles by staff writers and contributing editors from the total number of articles appearing in the magazine for a good idea of the percentage of free-lance material.

6. Check the Letters to the Editor. This may tell you what articles have run in some past issues and whether the magazine likes controversial ideas that spark reader comment.

7. Check the advertisements. A magazine without advertising usually depends on subscribers or private funding. Magazines with advertising will reveal much about their readership. Does the magazine advertise mostly automobiles and stereos, for example, or hand lotion and food? A magazine advertising expensive items usually means that the readership's income level is above average.

8. What is the magazine's audience? The descriptions in your marketing resources may tell you how sophisticated your audience is (age, education, and income levels are particularly useful); how large your audience is (a circulation figure of one million means your article must appeal to a wider audience); and how limited your audience is (whether, for instance, this magazine appeals specifically to midwestern computer operators or to all computer operators in the nation).

9. What types of articles does the magazine favor? Does the magazine run many profiles, how-tos, or personal experience pieces, for example? The type of article that appears most often will be the type of article for which you should query.

10. Does the magazine like famous personalities, either as interviewees or contributors? Are the articles by-lined only by national authorities? This will help you choose a profile topic or hint that you should seek authorities to quote for your article.

11. What is the length of each article? To figure this quickly, find a full page of type, count the number of words in one line, and multiply by the number of lines on the page. Each magazine is different, so do not use the multiplier from one magazine to estimate another. Although this is no absolute guide, you will be better able to match what the magazine says about article length with the magazine itself.

12. Are the sentences long or short? Are the paragraphs long or short? This will dictate the format for your article.

13. Does the magazine favor jargon over everyday language usage? Education publications may talk about ADA, for example, which the readers understand means Average Daily Attendance figures for children in school.

14. Check the theme of each article. Is it meant to inform, teach a moral, describe, or persuade?

15. Do photos accompany each article? Are the photos black-and-white or color? Do the photos show people or landscapes? Obviously this will tell you how to choose photo subjects to submit to each magazine.

Now that you better understand what current magazines are publishing and for what audience, you are ready to start focusing some ideas for your own articles.

FOR MORE INFORMATION

If a magazine to which you want to contribute is not in your library, you can request a sample copy. Send your request in care of the Editorial Department and enclose the price of a single issue plus postage. Also request any writer's guidelines the magazine may provide.

Haworth Press, 149 Fifth Avenue, New York, New York 10010, publishes several author's guides to specialized publications: *Journals in Business Administration and Management, Journals in Law, Criminal Justice and Criminology, Journals in Nursing, Journals in Psychology, Psychiatry and Social Work, Journals in Sociology and Related Fields,* and *Journals in the Health Field.*

The same people who publish *Writer's Market* publish a monthly magazine of marketing information, *Writer's Digest*, 9933 Alliance Road, Cincinnati, Ohio 45242. *The Writer*, 8 Arlington Street, Boston, Massachusetts 02116, issues a monthly magazine with marketing information and publishes *The Writer's Handbook*, with more than 100 chapters on free-lance writing and 2,500 markets. *The Freelancers Newsletter*, 307 Westlake Drive, Austin, Texas 78746, issues a bimonthly marketing update.

3

Focusing
Your Ideas

*I*t is impossible to teach you how to successfully market every idea
you have, but it is possible to teach you how to improve your
chance for success.

WHERE TO FIND SALABLE IDEAS

Your hobbies, your family's interests, and your occupation may
offer enough material to start a free-lance career. Clubs, churches,
and schools are other resources, as are friends and relatives. Of
course, a necessary part of any free-lancer's time is spent reading
magazines and newspapers to learn what is selling and to find
ideas. Good writers are usually voracious readers.

Newspaper stories can be divided into feature and news articles. An event that occurred yesterday and appears in the paper
today is a news item. Everything else is feature material, and a
majority of newspaper articles are features. Local news and fea-

tures are good sources of ideas, since an article about a local event or personality in an area newspaper may not have had national circulation.

To learn which newspapers publish in your vicinity, check *Editor and Publisher International Year Book*. This annual is the encyclopedia of the newspaper industry. Included are daily and weekly newspapers published in the United States, Canada, and foreign countries, as well as syndicates and industry organizations. This guide lists editors and circulation figures and devotes a special section to black newspapers and to foreign language newspapers printed in the United States.

For a broader view, the four major United States newspapers offer the key to topical information. You can begin your search for timely ideas outside of your own experience by reading the *New York Times*, the *Washington Post*, the *Los Angeles Times*, and the *Wall Street Journal*. The *New York Times*, the *Los Angeles Times*, and the *Post* publish daily (Sunday issues are especially full of feature ideas). The *Journal* is published Monday through Friday. All four are available at most libraries or by subscription.

Magazines are your marketplace, and familiarity with format and topics will make you a better seller. Subscribe to or read regularly magazines to which you would like to contribute articles. If a magazine is unavailable by subscription, write for a sample copy (see For More Information at the end of Chapter Two).

MAKING YOURSELF AVAILABLE

The more information you have, the more ideas you can market. Put yourself on as many mailing lists as possible. Associations, businesses, elected officials, government agencies, colleges, universities, chambers of commerce, and advertising agencies usually want to tell you what they are doing so you will write about them. Make yourself available by asking to be put on their mailing lists.

Your letter can say: "I am a free-lance writer covering issues that involve your organization. Would you please put me on your mailing list?" Begin by locating organizations and individuals using the following resources:

Associations

Encyclopedia of Associations is the only comprehensive source of trade associations, professional societies, labor unions, and fraternal and patriotic organizations. It contains nearly 15,000 listings with address and phone number, publications, as well as the name of the president. Lovers of the Stinking Rose, for instance, is an association of garlic lovers that "seeks to protect garlic in all its varied functions around the world. Lobbies against mouthwash companies and others who disparage garlic and its rich odor."

Businesses

Standard and Poor's Register of Corporations, Directors and Executives is published annually in three volumes. Volume 1 lists American corporations alphabetically; Volume 2 shows directors and executives; Volume 3 indexes Volumes 1 and 2, including a very helpful geographic listing of corporations by states and major cities.

Dunn and Bradstreet Reference Book of Corporate Managements, a biennial, includes a more detailed listing of public relations people, with educational backgrounds. It is issued less frequently than *Standard and Poor's.*

Elected Officials and Government Agencies

The Federal Directory, updated semiannually, lists federal employees by name and agency. The focus is Washington, D. C., with business addresses and phone numbers. It shows members of Congress and details agency bureaucrats.

Taylor's Encyclopedia of Government Officials includes federal and state officers. It may not be available in smaller libraries, but this loose-leaf directory is the most comprehensive resource tool on public officials, updated monthly with legislation signed by the president, as well as proclamations and executive orders issued.

Colleges and Universities

Education Directory, Colleges and Universities is an annual that catalogs community colleges, as well as four-year colleges and universities. No public relations people are shown, but call the phone number listed and ask for the name so you can address your request personally to the Public Information Officer.

Chambers of Commerce

Ari's Chamber of Commerce Directory is updated periodically with addresses and phone numbers, as well as publications of each organization (U.S. only).

Johnson's World Wide Chamber of Commerce Directory shows the same information as *Ari's*, but this is for principal foreign as well as American cities.

Advertising Agencies

Standard Directory of Advertisers, an annual, classifies advertisers by types of products they sell—shoes, for example. It lists company name, address, and phone, some top executives, and the name of the advertising agency that handles each company's account.

Standard Directory of Advertising Agencies, a biannual, classifies advertising agencies alphabetically along with the accounts they manage.

Above all, advertise yourself. When you talk with friends, listen to them for possible ideas, but also make sure to mention you are writing regularly. Personal contacts often are the most fruitful.

Is this stealing? No. Ideas cannot be copyrighted. You are only borrowing a concept. Your definition and compilation of that concept will be *your* article, different from the information you collect. "I steal from everybody" should be your motto, as long as you are only stealing ideas.

Will you need an agent? In a word, no. Agents rarely work with beginning free-lancers, and usually handle magazine articles only in conjunction with an upcoming book from which the agent can market excerpts. Agents can be helpful people (who commonly receive ten percent for their services), but wait until you are ready to market a book before searching for an agent. *Literary Market Place* publishes a listing of agents (See Chapter Two).

IDEAS VS. TOPICS

When you say "I want to write an article about television news," you have an idea. Ideas, by themselves, do not make good magazine articles. Obviously, the concept is too broad, and a magazine editor approached by a writer with this idea will reply: "What do you want to say about television news?"

The refinement of this idea can be called a topic. If you are an able free-lancer, your reply will be an article entitled "Disco News," an analysis of the deterioration of local television news by Edwin Diamond in the *Washington Journalism Review*.

The general idea is always less appealing to an editor than the specific. An editor may spend time with a veteran contributor to define an idea into a topic, but editors will be less patient with newcomers. So, your idea must be refined when it reaches the editor.

To test whether you have an idea or a topic, try to state your idea as a question and an answer. If one question and one answer cover your idea, you probably have a refined article. The question asked by Diamond's article is "What is the current quality of local television news?" The answer, according to Diamond, is that local television news is "practically all entertainment, and practically zero information."

TYPES OF ARTICLES

Magazine articles tend to fall into ten categories. None of these categories is exclusive, and sometimes they overlap. You could write a historical travel article, for instance, or an inspirational profile. Once you know the categories, however, you can match your idea with its category and then with the markets that buy articles in that category.

Informational article. This is the most common. An informational article may sketch a runner's map for your town, describe a medical procedure, or detail parts of a 1936 Ford engine.

How-to. An easily recognizable how-to is the recipe. However, recipes for solar water heaters are just as much how-tos as recipes for Hot Texas Chili, and more marketable. How-tos are a good choice for the beginning free-lancer.

Profile. In the 1920s, the *New Yorker* magazine popularized the idea that a magazine article could sketch a word portrait of a personality, and that section of the magazine was called "Profile." Interviews with notable people are always salable, but a profile of someone in your community with an unusual hobby or profession or someone who has accomplished an interesting feat is just as marketable. This is another good choice for the novice.

Historical. This type of article is not confined to historical events or people, but simply describes an article arranged chronologically to reveal facts, whether you are describing the history of the hot dog or chronicling the events that caused the 1929 stock market crash.

Personal experience. A common element of any personal experience article is the pronoun "I," since the storyteller is usually the central observer. Everyday personal experiences often make good fiction when told well, but for nonfiction you are more likely to sell an adventure that few people have shared.

Inspirational. This is a variety of the personal experience article, although the experience may be a friend's or a relative's. A moral message is crucial here.

Humor and satire. This is a difficult form, mastered by few. If you want to try, do not write a letter to an editor asking whether he or she would be interested in your humor. Send the entire article. This is different from all other types of articles, where you query the editor first.

Travel. Visiting Waikiki may have been fascinating for you, but asking a travel editor to buy 6,000 words about "gorgeous white sand beaches" is an insult. The successful travel writer chooses the offbeat, photographs the unusual, visits the out-of-the-way.

Investigative. An evolutionary form of what was called "muckraking" at the turn-of-the-century, investigative articles are time-consuming and rely heavily on detailed research. The beginning free-lancer should avoid this type of article, as the markets are limited and the money you receive for your article may not compensate for the time and money you must spend gathering statistics. However, if you are already a specialist in a subject area, have completed the research as part of another project, and know that no investigation of the same type has been published, this can be satisfying and lucrative.

Point-of-view. The Letters to the Editor column of every newspaper contains someone's point of view. If you want to sound off on a topic, write a Letter to the Editor and do not expect to be paid for it. In this category, editors are especially impressed by titles. Free-lancers should avoid this type of article unless they have an extraordinary background and are themselves experts or they have personal access to experts whom they can quote to support a point-of-view article. Marketable point-of-view articles usually contain opinions by people credentialed to state those opinions.

HOW TO DO A TOPIC ANALYSIS

If you planned to sell your car, you would probably first figure out who were likely buyers and who would pay the best price. A magazine article idea is a commodity like a car, and as a free-lancer you must know your likely buyers and what price to expect. A topic analysis helps you focus your ideas, tells you where articles on your topics have appeared, teaches you who is buying what ideas regularly, and whether a magazine has just run an article you were planning to query. Start with five different magazine ideas and check where and when articles on a topic similar to yours ran during the last two years.

Reader's Guide to Periodical Literature is where most free-lancers start when they want to check what is being published on a topic. Since 1900, *Reader's Guide* has catalogued by author and subject many articles in most general interest magazines. The list of magazines indexed is at the beginning of each volume. This is a good starting point, but just a beginning. Many lesser known periodical indexes will guide you to more specific information.

Agriculture Index (1919 to date) indexes periodicals in agriculture, forestry, botany, and horticulture.

Applied Science and Technology Index (1913 to date) indexes periodicals covering aeronautics and space science, computer technology, engineering, and the food and textile industries.

Art Index (1929 to date) indexes periodicals covering archaeology, architecture, ceramics, graphic arts, painting, and sculpture.

Business Periodicals Index (1958 to date, preceded by *Industrial Arts Index*, 1913–1957) indexes advertising, business, finance, labor, taxation, and marketing articles.

Education Index (1929 to date) indexes educational literature, including bulletins and reports, and also includes articles on educational psychology.

Social Sciences and Humanities Index (formerly *International Index*, 1907–1974) covers scholarly journals in the humanities and social sciences. In June 1974, it divided into the *Social Sciences Index* (1974 to date) covering economics, geography, law, criminology, and medical sciences, and *Humanities Index* (1974 to date), which includes language, literature, performing arts, religion, theology, and philosophy.

Counterculture movements, prominent in the 1970s, spawned indexes of their own. *Reader's Guide* does not index *Crawdaddy* magazine, for instance, but *Popular Periodicals Index* does. Two other indexes that catalog articles from popular culture magazines are *The New Periodicals Index* and *Access. Abstracts of Popular Cultu,e* catalogs, as well as prints, excerpts from many magazines not found in traditional periodicals guides. Check each index for a listing of the periodicals included.

If, after checking the appropriate indexes, you can find only a few articles written recently on your topic, you may have a new idea, something the magazines have not been queried about before. This is a good sign.

If you find regular listings for your idea, your topic is probably overdone, but perhaps you can think of a new angle on an old idea. Or you may find that a magazine regularly runs a staff-written feature on your idea, which certainly knocks that magazine off your query list. This search can also give you several resources for your article and a head start on your research. Now that you know what each magazine is using, you can better decide which ideas you can take to market.

4

A New Approach
to Marketing

*M*ultiple markets should be your goal. Why should you do extensive research, spend a month or more of your time, just to sell one article? A better approach is to find topics that will satisfy more than one buyer.

MARKET CATEGORIES

Magazine markets in a guide like *Writer's Market* or *Magazine Industry Market Place* divide magazines into market categories— women's, sports, and science magazines, for example. A good magazine article is one you can sell in more than one market category and to more than one magazine in each category.

You might have a topic, such as how to make a needlepoint pillow, which you believe would appeal to women's magazines. You can find three potential women's magazines to whom you can send your topic. But if none of them wants your topic, you are stuck. You cannot transfer the topic to another market category because its appeal is too limited.

SLANTING YOUR TOPIC

A successful topic that can fit into more than one category, for example, might be an article about women who lift weights as part of a university physical fitness experiment. This can be written from a news angle for a local newspaper ("This is what these women are doing now"), from a sports angle for a sports magazine ("This experiment may help women become better athletic competitors"), or for a science magazine ("This controlled, documented experiment may tell us something about how women respond physiologically to regular heavy exercise").

With three different market categories you can take three different article approaches with one central topic. Each approach is called a "slant." This means you will tailor your article to fit each of the different subject category magazines.

A story about a retired television executive who runs a one-man cable television station, for instance, can be slanted to interest retirees (retirement market category), businesspeople (business and finance category), or people who live in the television station's radius (regional category).

Each of these audiences for the article topic would want to know about different aspects of this man's business. The retirees might want to know how much time he spends working, how he started the business, what kinds of people he meets. Businesspeople might want to know how much money he needed to start the television station, how many subscribe to the cable service, how much it costs to run the station, and how much profit he expects. Area residents might want to know about his personality, how long he has lived in the area, what he does when he is not on television, and what local events he plans to cover. Basically, the story is the same, but the slant—the approach, the tailoring of the information—requires different emphasis for each different audience.

PRIMARY, SECONDARY, AND TERTIARY MARKETS

Besides falling into market categories, magazines can be classified into categories according to how much they pay. Magazines that pay more than $400 for an article can be considered primary markets; magazines that pay less than $400 but more than $150 are secondary markets; magazines that pay less, including those that pay writers only in complimentary copies, can be called tertiary markets.

Because of the rate of pay and either their prestige (*Harper's* or *The Atlantic Monthly*), wide readership (*Parade* or *Reader's Digest*), or both prestige and wide readership, primary magazines attract notable talent. Many of them, however, still look constantly for new writers to add to their list of contributors. The beginning free-lancer need not fear these markets and should always try to include them in any queries, but this cannot be the anchor of your free-lance career. For this, you are lucky to have the secondary and tertiary markets.

Secondary markets include some fine magazines with smaller audiences than those in the primary markets. Special subject magazines often fall into this category (such as magazines for skiers or runners), as do magazines targeted for certain age levels (such as children or retirees).

Tertiary market editors often simply do not have the money to pay more than $150 for any article, and they sometimes accept reprinted material (material that has already appeared several times in other magazines not circulated to their audiences), in addition to new material solicited from free-lancers.

Tertiary magazines usually have small staffs and, therefore, accept more free-lance material than secondary or primary markets. They can also be good markets for recirculated material, articles you have sold elsewhere in primary or secondary markets, which do not compete with tertiary market circulation. Many religious magazines are good examples of noncompeting markets, since the editor of a Baptist publication can assume that not too many Baptist readers will follow a Catholic publication.

Local newspapers are another tertiary market often overlooked. On a large newspaper, section editors purchase material for each section, such as sports or book reviews; smaller newspapers may have one or two editors who control the content.

Writing for local newspapers also gives you the advantage of visibility and credibility in your community. When you ask for an interview, your name may be familiar, which makes your job easier. Investigate this market in your town. Never overlook it.

MULTIPLE MARKETING

A marketable topic can be defined as one with a potential audience in at least three market categories, to at least three magazines in each of these categories. This means you must be able to slant your single topic to a variety of audiences. Turn an interview with a female Olympic skier into an article for: (1) skiing magazines (slanted to emphasize her technique), (2) sport trade magazines (slanted to emphasize marketing approaches to selling her equipment), and (3) women's magazines (slanted to emphasize her personality and determination).

In each of these magazine market categories, you can find three magazines that might be interested. In the first category, you can try *Ski, Ski America,* and *Skiing Magazine.* In the second, you can try *Ski Business, Skiing Trade News,* and *Sports Merchandiser.* Category three offers *Cosmopolitan, Ms.,* and *McCall's.* Each slant should include at least one primary market, if possible, but some magazine categories do not contain markets that pay $400 or more.

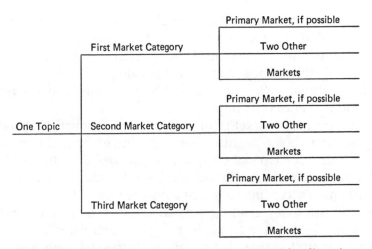

Diagram 1 *A marketable topic is one that has a potential audience in at least three market categories, to at least three magazines in each of these categories.*

By trying three magazines in each category, you have nine potential markets, and you multiply your chance to succeed with a single idea nine times.

You will not always be able to follow this "nine market" rule. Sometimes your article will have a limited audience of, perhaps, two categories, and you will want to research the topic simply because you like it or because the article will be easy to do. But the topics truly worth pursuing with your time and energy are those with at least a nine market potential.

This approach is called a multiple query system—sending more than one query on each topic. Do not confuse this with multiple submissions, which means sending one completed article to more than one magazine at the same time. Multiple submissions are not recommended, since you risk two different editors using the same material simultaneously, which will not make you welcome the next time you submit an article.

Multiple queries risk little. You simply ask more than one editor at a time whether your idea will fit, just as you would show that mythical car you were selling to all interested buyers.

"What do I do if I get nine positive answers?" you ask. The answer is that you are not going to get nine positive answers. For one reason or another, some of the magazines will not need your idea at this time. They may have a backlog of articles, they may have just run an article on a related topic, or they may not recognize the brilliance of your proposal.

If a primary market returns a positive response, that should be your first choice because that magazine will pay the most, or because its wide circulation will give you visibility. If, instead, a secondary or tertiary market shows interest, you can choose among them according to which pays the most.

You can delay sending your article to your second or third choice until you have an answer to your completed manuscript from your first choice. If you are unsuccessful with your first choice, you still have a second, perhaps a third chance. Once your article has been accepted in one category, you can write any remaining interested magazines in that category, thanking them for their interest and explaining that another magazine has bought your article.

Diagram 2 *Turn an interview with a female Olympic skier into an article for: (1) skiing magazines (slanted to emphasize her technique), (2) sport trade magazines (slanted to emphasize marketing approaches to selling her equipment), and (3) women's magazines (slanted to emphasize her personality and determination).*

		Ski (secondary market)
	(1) Skiing Magazines	*Ski America* (secondary market)
		Skiing Magazine (secondary market)
		Skiing Trade News (secondary market)
Female Olympic Skier	(2) Sport Trade Magazines	*Sports Merchandiser* (secondary market)
		Ski Business (tertiary market)
		Cosmopolitan (primary market)
	(3) Women's Magazines	*Ms.* (secondary market)
		McCall's (primary market)

Do not forget that this is just in one market category for one of the slants you planned for the article. Each of your other two market categories may also contain magazines that want the article, so you have multiplied the efficiency of the time you spend researching what is essentially one article times your nine potential markets.

This selective system of marketing—sending only those ideas that the writer has carefully screened—reduces time and paper load and increases the chances that magazines will receive more usable material from competent writers. This approach also increases the writer's odds for making a sale and puts the writer more in control of the markets.

5

How to Write an Effective Query

*T*hink of your query as a letter of introduction. You will probably never meet the editor to whom you are writing, yet you are asking in your query for editorial time, patience, and eventually money.

Do not think you can avoid the query process by telephoning an editor for a quick reaction. Few editors answer calls from unfamiliar free-lancers, and often your idea must be reviewed by several editors before it is approved. A letter is much easier to evaluate. Only after you have worked with a specific editor for some time will a telephone call for a go-ahead become possible.

Since some editors often receive 100 or more queries in one day, your query, first, must be technically flawless—no spelling or punctuation errors, no grammatical mistakes, no typographical errors. "Half the queries I get look like they were written and typed by third-graders," one editor complained. "If the query isn't neat and organized, I'm likely to reject it."

Second, like the article you will eventually write, the query must rivet the editor's attention. Your idea must sound better than the other ninety-nine queries on the editor's desk that day. To do this, your query must be well thought out and must reflect the detailed care that you will eventually give your article.

Before you begin to write your query, assemble some statistics, make some preliminary contacts, gather enough material to make your query sound authoritative. When you ask for information from other people, explain that you are gathering the data so you can query editors about an article. This generally makes people very willing to help you sell your idea to the editors. Do not do exhaustive research on your topic until you have buyers.

QUERY CHECKLIST

The next step is to review the following checklist:

Topicality. Has the topic been overdone? Is your approach too familiar? A current topic is the best kind, but cover it differently than other articles on the same subject. Mining for gold is always a good article idea, but detailing how to dive for gold with scuba gear is much more salable.

Scope. Will you promise in your query to explain too much? Remember that few magazines run articles longer than 2,000 words, or eight double-spaced, typed pages. Make sure you limit the scope of your topic so you can cover the subject in eight pages or less, depending on your market.

Time. Will you have time in your schedule to complete the article competently? Will you have to travel or do several interviews? How much research is necessary? If this is a visual story, can you take the pictures, or must you hire a photographer? Ideally, an article should take no more than four to six weeks to put together from conception to completion.

Access. Will you be able to interview and collect your information easily, or will there be delays? Must you seek information under the Freedom of Information Act (see Chapter Seven), for instance, or will your interviewees be on vacation when you want to see them? With controversial articles and/or notable public figures, these are important considerations.

Money. Will your expenses to do this story exceed the fees you will be paid for the article? Sometimes publishing an important article supercedes this pecuniary thought, but be realistic.

FORMAT FOR YOUR QUERY

Your query letter should be typed (never hand-written) on 8½ x 11 white twenty-pound bond paper. Do not use erasable paper, which smudges too easily. Leave one-inch margins on all sides, center your letter well, and make a carbon copy for your records. Whether to use letterhead is a small controversy among freelancers. If you decide you want letterhead, allow enough time for printing.

A query letter should never be longer than one page, single-spaced, with double spaces between paragraphs. Think of that busy editor with all that mail, and ask yourself whether you would read beyond the first page.

The letter should be appropriately addressed "Dear Mr./Mrs./Miss/Ms." If you cannot tell how to address the editor from the market listing, use the whole name, such as "Dear Sandy Brown." If no editor is listed, check the publication masthead for the editor's name. A query addressed simply "Dear Editor" will be about as successful as a letter addressed "Occupant."

Eight Rules About Style

1. Be conversational. Write the query as you would a letter to an acquaintance, but not a close friend. Stilted language in a query will hint that your forthcoming article will be just as stark. So, unless you are querying an academic publication, favor common usage over formal style—use "you" instead of "one" (as in "One should find this interesting"), for example, and "house" instead of "residence."

2. Avoid unnecessary introductory self-apparent thoughts, such as "I am a free-lance writer who . . ." or apologies such as "I know you will probably think this is a silly article idea, but . . ."

3. Maintain a consistent theme. Omit any sentence or idea that does not directly clarify your central idea. Suggest only one article idea in each letter.

4. Do not assume too much. Avoid technical jargon or abbreviations your editor might not recognize—"graph" for "paragraph" or "b.p." for boiling point, for example.

5. Favor short sentences (twenty-five words or less) over long ones. Divide a complex long sentence into two shorter sentences. Also be alert for unnecessary words that can be omitted without changing your meaning. "He was born in a log cabin, and by the time he was six he was reading the tales of Shakespeare and Proust," can become "He was born in a log cabin. At six, he was reading Shakespeare and Proust."

6. Favor the specific over the general. Rather than saying "I would like to write an article about octupi," say "Baby octupi are being born for the first time in captivity at Sierra College in northern California."

7. Convey action and description. Rather than "One would thoroughly enjoy a trip to the village of Koloa, Kauai," say "In Koloa, Kauai, you can buy a banana 'shave ice'—banana-flavored crushed ice perched on a giant scoop of banana ice cream in a paper cone."

8. Limit your query to four carefully planned paragraphs. Each paragraph should contain one idea, based on your central theme. Your first paragraph is the most important because many editors stop after the first few sentences if your idea does not shout at them right away. A well-prepared query that commands attention can keep you out of Vonzaa Derrick's hobby club:

Unintentionally, I have become a collector! Although my objective had been to write great novels and other masterpieces, I suddenly realized that I possessed the world's largest and most complete collection of rejection slips. Riffling through my assortment, I have decided upon an entirely new field. Henceforth, I will be the first rejection slip critic!

No one can deny my qualifications. In this area, I have no peer. As there are no college courses in rejection slip criticism, none can claim superior academic achievements. In sheer volume, I reign supreme.

I intend to be fair in my judgment and not influenced by the fact that one magazine has rejected me five to one over the challengers. My appraisal will be based wholly upon the quality of content.

I should first like to commend all of the editors on their courtesy. This is a sterling trait, and you have all responded laudably. Thank you for your thank-yous.

A word about the overall material content. It is trite and repetitious. Please strive for originality and a fresh approach. The hackneyed report will never make it here. I am seeking that rejection slip which has something to offer the reader—something bespeaking literary excellence.

A standard rejection slip consists of the following components: "One or more editors have read the material," "We regret that it does not suit our needs," "Due to the volume of material received it is impossible to make individual comments." These are usually cheaply printed and unsigned.

These forms are far too sterile and impersonal, and therefore, will never make the top ten in my rejection slip awards. You must bear in mind that a writer is like a wounded little bird, needing love and the feeling that you care.

As stated previously, several publications make a point of stressing, "Your manuscript has been read by one or more editors." Perhaps they should add, "wearing white gloves." Can you appreciate the joy of seeing a ketchup spot on page three? The ecstatic glee of finding a cigar burn on page 12? My manuscripts are returned in spotless condition, the only evidence of their having been seen by one or more editors being the absence of my paper clip. I am already making a significant contribution to the economy by supporting the Postal Service. Regardless of the merit of the rejection slip, points will be deducted for pilfered paper clips.

Sincerity is, of course, an essential quality. Most editors miss the boat by not realizing that the rejectee is a warm, real person. Therefore, the rejection slip is often tart, crisp and plastic. In my vast collection of 9,738 slips reading "We regret that we are unable to use the enclosed material," there are only four on which editors took the trouble to personalize. One wrote, "Thanks, but not for us." Blunt, harsh, but treasured because a human being operated that pen. Another responded with the singular, "Sorry!" but this was a magazine with an enormous circulation and I was touched. Yet another commented, "This is good, but I'm afraid we don't have a spot for it." That a check had not fluttered to the floor was insignificant. Because an editor of obvious taste and discernment had noted that it was good. The fourth, an absolute genius, stated, "Brilliant! Unfortunately it does not suit our needs." A writer can derive sustenance to tide him over the next 30 rejections from such an appraisal. These are the editors I value highly because they communicated wisdom, compassion, and a genuine sorrow that I couldn't be immortalized by them.

The past decade has wrought tremendous change and in all this state of flux only two things remain static, bacteria and rejection slips.

One magazine, which has been consistently rejecting me for 15 years, conveys its message on a plain white unlined file card. In all the years of our correspondence it has changed neither in phraseology nor appearance. As a loyal rejectee, I am disappointed at this publication's lack of initiative in upgrading its form. The "recipe card" should be abandoned, to be replaced by something with a border of bright daisies, peeking forth from a background of lilting lilacs. Or, smiling faces, clustered around the corners in a jubilant yellow.

Certainly the prose should be altered to something less formal, more friendly. Like, "Well, you're trying again, you little devil." Or, "Hey, are you still mailing?" The writer knows that he has been recognized, and recognition is vitally important.

An annual revision of the form could become a conversation piece among rejectees. "Have you got the 1974 Saturday Evening Post slip? I think it's the best of my new lot." Or: "I'm really disappointed in my '74 Reader's Digest. They've reprinted the '73 Farm Journal."

The advantage of my collection is of a dual nature. For me, it means looking forward to each new rejection slip. Perhaps there will be a novel, imaginative jewel for my exciting new hobby. For the editor, it presents the challenging opportunity to compete with equally astute professionals for superior achievement in a heretofore unappreciated field.

Furthermore, I am forming a club so that rejection slip collectors may exchange with one another. Somewhat on the order of baseball card trading, *this activity will aid writers who may be glutted with one publication's rejections and sadly lacking in others. They may thereby achieve more well-rounded collections.* As a starter, I have three Good Housekeeping's *that I will trade for one* National Geographic. *For you nostalgia buffs, what would you give for a genuine* Liberty?[1]

MODEL QUERIES

A query can begin with a short anecdote or quotation demonstrating your idea, a straight statement of fact that explains your proposal, or an expansion of a news item. Sample queries follow.

Paragraph One. Begin right away with your idea. The first sentence should be a grabby beginning that cannot be ignored. Remember—you are selling and writing at the same time.

1. Anecdote with a quotation.

Shirley Boccaccio's second-story flat sits on a hill in the midst of what was once the Haight-Ashbury flower child pheonomenon. The neighborhood now houses an assortment of students, homosexuals, lesbians, minorities, young marrieds, single parents, and children. "You know, I have to feel this is the best place my children could grow up," Shirley said, looking out the window at the rain.

This is grabby because your editor wants to know how this woman could possibly feel that Haight-Ashbury is a good place for her children.

2. Factual beginning.

In California, twenty-three university students lift fifty-pound weights three times a week in a weightlifting class. This doesn't sound exceptional, but these twenty-three students are all women.

An unexpected combination of facts grabs the editor here.

3. News beginning.

Sarah S. was acquitted of murder today after a month-long trial, even though four people testified they watched her kill her husband with a revolver on the front lawn of their Phoenix home. Mrs. Shroeder's defense was a new medical examination called a psychiatric autopsy.

Here the news value of the story—both as a murder trial and as a new defense—combine to invite attention.

Paragraph Two. Here is an opportunity to expand on your topic, to explain further what you propose.

1. Second paragraph for Boccaccio query.

At age thirty, divorced from her first husband, Shirley yearned to have a family. So, this former beauty contest winner handpicked a man she had known for ten years to father her children. They agreed they would not marry. Penelope, now six, was the firstborn. Then came Peter, four, and Charlie, two.

2. Second paragraph for weightlifting query.

These twenty-three women, with an average weight of 125 pounds, are participating in an experimental program at the University of California at Davis. Program Director Jack Wilmore hopes to learn whether women can use weightlifting to control their figures without becoming muscle-bound

3. Second paragraph for murder query.

A psychiatric autopsy attempts to profile the victim to determine circumstances that may have provoked the murderer. In Mrs. S.'s case, through extensive interviews with friends and relatives, examiners determined that Mr. S. consistently beat his wife and often threatened their children. Jurors said they felt the murder was a kind of retaliatory self-defense.

Paragraph Three. Here list your qualifications to write the article if you are an expert in your field. In the weightlifting story, for example, if you were the doctor doing the tests, you would say so. But more often you are writing *about* someone else who is an expert or who is doing something newsworthy. In that case, overlook any reference to your expertise (or lack of it) and state the title of the article you propose, the length of the article (check specifications for the publication), and whether you can provide photographs. If the article is timely, indicate when you can have the manuscript ready.

1. Third paragraph of Boccaccio query.

I can prepare a 1,000-word article, "San Franciscan Devoted to Role of Mother, Not Wife," with color photographs, based on Shirley Boccaccio's decision to have children, but not to marry.

2. Third paragraph of weightlifting query.

The weightlifting experiment has lasted about a month now and will conclude in six weeks. I can prepare for your readers a 1,000-word article, "Women Who Lift Weights," with black-and-white photographs.

3. Third paragraph of murder query. (Note the change for added expertise and newsworthiness.)

As the psychiatrist who directed the psychiatric autopsy for the trial, I feel I have a perspective that would help your readers understand this new procedure. For fifteen years I have practiced psychiatric medicine at Mercy Hospital in San Francisco. I can have a 3,000-word article, "Psychiatric Autopsy–the New Defense Against Murder," ready in two weeks to take advantage of the issue's topicality.

Paragraph Four. This paragraph should ideally be a short question, which reminds the editor that you would like a quick response.

1. Fourth paragraph for Boccaccio query.

Is __(name of publication)__ interested in an article on this living experiment with feminism?

2. Fourth paragraph for weightlifting query.

Is __(name of publication)__ interested in an article on these pioneering women when the class ends and the statistics are compiled?

3. Fourth paragraph for murder query.

Is __(name of publication)__ interested in an article explaining the details of this new defense technique?

See samples of completed queries at the end of this chapter.

Speak Softly and Carry a Beagle, A Peanuts Parade Book, (New York: Holt, Rinehart, 1974), p. 9. © 1974, 1975 United Feature Syndicate, Inc.

ELEVEN COMMON QUERY MISTAKES

Some of these common query mistakes may seem ludicrous, but all are gathered from editors' actual experiences.

1. Don't include too much information. This is the most common error in writing queries; it leaves little new material for the manuscript and aggravates the editor with little time to spend weaving through too many facts at once. Leave some surprises, or there is no reason for the editor to want to see your manuscript.

2. Don't oversell your idea. Do not write your query like an advertising copywriter, with several imperative sentences, such as "Your readers can't wait another minute to hear the details of my article!" Just like a salesperson who sticks a foot in your front door before it slams, the pushy query writer is offensive. Be confident, not overzealous.

3. Don't tell the editor how much your mother/father/dog/cat/horse enjoy your writing. The editor's opinion is the only important one.

4. Don't say "Your magazine usually doesn't publish articles on this subject, but you should, so here's my idea." Converting the editor to a new editorial policy is not your job.

5. Don't threaten the editor. "I dare you to publish this" will probably get a very cold response.

6. Don't tell the editor that your psychological well-being depends on this article being published, or that your next meal depends on the success of your article. Using this tactic guarantees that you will remain psychologically unfit and starving.

7. Don't mention names you think will impress the editor, such as "When I was talking with Hunter the other day—that's Hunter Thompson, you know." First, you risk that the editor does not know who Hunter Thompson is. Second, the editor may not like Hunter Thompson or any other person you feel would impress. Avoid this amateurism.

8. Don't use footnotes. This may be fine for your college term paper, but few magazines use footnotes, and your query should not contain them either.

9. Don't send writing samples with your query. They make your letter too bulky and are also easily misplaced and not returned. You may mention as part of your qualifications that you have written articles on the same topic, naming specific magazines where your articles have appeared.

10. Don't offer premiums as enticement to use your article. "My brother/aunt/friend can get you two free tickets to go with me to the next Central City Fair" means you lack confidence in your article topic. It also means you will be going to the fair alone.

11. Don't send candy, knitted socks, sliced salami, or any other gift as an attention-getter. Bright stickers and illustrations on the outside of your envelope also fall into this category. A good idea can stand scrutiny on its own and does not need any help.

Now, carefully read your finished queries for content and typographical and spelling errors. Always keep a copy of each query, filed by topic, for your records. Sign your name and put your query in a number 10 rectangular envelope. Include an SASE (refer to abbreviations in Chapter Two); a number 9 envelope fits nicely inside, or fold a number 10 to fit. Mail individually typed queries to each of the nine magazines you have chosen for each of your topics—three magazines in at least three different market categories (see Chapter Four). For three topics, this would mean twenty-seven queries you could drop in the mailbox at once. Now you wait.

"How long must I wait?" you ask impatiently. Four to six weeks is not an uncommon response time. Larger magazines tend to take longer because of the amount of mail they receive. If you have not heard from a magazine after six weeks, write a reminder note. It is unusual that a magazine does not respond at all.

While you are sitting there next to the mailbox, you can read the next chapter and get organized to start your article.

Sample 1 *Query with Anecdote and Quotation*

> Address
> City, State, Zip
> Phone (with area code)
> Date

Editor's Name
Publication
Street Address
City, State, Zip

Dear (Editor's Name) :

   Shirley Boccaccio's second-story flat sits on a hill in the midst of what was once the Haight-Ashbury flower child phenomenon. The neighborhood now houses an assortment of students, homosexuals, lesbians, minorities, young marrieds, single parents, and children. "You know, I have to feel this is the best place my children could grow up," Shirley said, looking out the window at the rain.

   At age thirty, divorced from her first husband, Shirley yearned to have a family. So, this former beauty contest winner handpicked a man she had known for ten years to father her children. They agreed they would not marry. Penelope, now six, was the firstborn. Then came Peter, four, and Charlie, two.

I can prepare a 1,000-word article, "San Franciscan Devoted to Role of Mother, Not Wife," with color photographs, based on Shirley Boccaccio's decision to have children, but not to marry.

Is (name of publication) interested in an article on this living experiment with feminism?

Cordially,

Your Name

Sample 2 *Factual Query*

Street Address
City, State, Zip
Phone (with area code)
Date

Editor's Name
Publication
Street Address
City, State, Zip

Dear (Editor's Name) :

In California, twenty-three university students lift fifty-pound weights three times a week in a weightlifting class. This doesn't sound exceptional, but these twenty-three students are all women.

These twenty-three women, with an average weight of 125 pounds, are participating in an experimental program at the University of California at Davis. Program Director Jack Wilmore hopes to learn whether women can use weightlifting to control their figures without becoming muscle-bound.

The weightlifting experiment has lasted about a month now, and will conclude in six weeks. I can prepare for your readers a 1,000 word article, "Women Who Lift Weights," with black-and-white photographs.

Is _(name of publication)_ interested in an article on these pioneering women when the class ends and the statistics are compiled?

Cordially,

Your Name

Sample 3 *News Query*

Street Address
City, State, Zip
Phone (with area code)
Date

Editor's Name
Publication
Street Address
City, State, Zip

Dear _(Editor's Name)_:

Sarah S. was acquitted of murder today after a month-long trial, even though four people testified they watched her kill her husband with a revolver in front of their Phoenix home. Mrs. S.'s defense was a new medical examination called a psychiatric autopsy.

A psychiatric autopsy attempts to profile the victim to determine circumstances that may have provoked the murderer. In Mrs. S.'s case, through extensive interviews with friends and relatives, examiners determined that Mr. S. consistently beat his wife and often threatened their children. Jurors said they felt the murder was a kind of retaliatory self-defense.

As the psychiatrist who directed the psychiatric autopsy for the trial, I feel I have a perspective that would help your readers understand this new procedure. For fifteen years I have practiced psychiatric medicine at Mercy Hospital in San Francisco. I can have a 3,000-word article,

"Psychiatric Autopsy—the New Defense Against Murder," ready in two weeks to take advantage of the issue's topicality.

Is __(name of publication)__ interested in an article explaining the details of this new defense technique?

Cordially,

Your Name

6

Organizing to Start Your Article

*O*rganizing to write a magazine article is like packing a suitcase—you can pack neatly so you can retrieve what you need when you need it, or you can throw everything in and hope you will be able to find what you want when you arrive. Following are some hints to help you pack neatly.

GATHERING SUPPLIES

Before you even begin research, prepare yourself to write. This will avoid all those last-minute trips to the store for supplies. Scissors, cellophane tape, and an eraser are a writer's essential tools. They indicate a willingness to reconsider, to reflect, to rewrite.

Besides these sophisticated editing implements, you should have:

1. What Virginia Woolf called "A Room of One's Own." This need not be an actual room, but you must have a space to collect material and to write that is separate from the rest of your house or apartment. This can be a table in the den or a desk with a file drawer to keep your research. Constantly retrieving supplies and files from a closet upsets thought patterns and organization. Find a separate place for yourself.

2. A typewriter and a typewriter table. You probably already gathered these to type your query. When all those checks start filling your mailbox, also buy a secretarial chair to avoid backache.

3. Manila file folders and, if possible, a two-drawer file. Label separate files for research, interviews, correspondence, and photographs with different colored labels so you can retrieve them quickly.

4. Twenty-pound 8½ x 11 paper for your manuscripts. You should have some left over from querying. Again, do not buy erasable paper because it smudges.

5. Scratch 8½ x 11 paper for first/second/third drafts (preferably a different color than white so you will not confuse final and rough drafts).

6. A calendar, month-at-a-glance or flipover desk type, to keep track of your appointments and deadlines.

7. Some 9 x 12 manila envelopes for mailing manuscripts. Save thick cardboard and cut to 8½" x 11" size to fit inside the envelope to protect your manuscripts for mailing.

8. Address labels for the manila envelopes and return address stickers.

9. Some 3 x 5 notecards for library research (see Chapter Seven).

10. A writing tablet, letter or legal size, to keep a list of the contacts you make, and a stenographer's notepad for interview notes.

11. A new typewriter ribbon to replace the one that wears out at midnight in the middle of a line.

12. Carbon paper, typewriter correcting tape and fluid, paper clips, pencils, pens, and stamps.

13. A mileage record book (see Appendix A).

14. A tape recorder (if you use one) with sixty-minute cassettes and a plug. (If you are a photographer, see Chapter Nine for a list of supplies.)

15. Patience.

Tools do not a good writer make, but organization helps. To save trips to the library, a free-lancer should gradually assemble a comprehensive home reference library. Basic reference tools are listed below.

HOME REFERENCE LIBRARY

1. A dictionary, such as:

American Heritage Dictionary of the English Language (American Heritage). Includes many slang and colloquial words. Larger in size than the usual desk dictionary.

Webster's New Collegiate Dictionary (Merriam). Based on standard usage, with some slang and colloquialisms included.

2. A thesaurus, such as:

Roget's International Thesaurus (Crowell). Arranged alphabetically according to general categories of ideas. Available in paperback.

Webster's Collegiate Thesaurus (Merriam). More than 100,000 synonyms, antonyms, and idiomatic phrases, listed alphabetically.

3. A language usage guide (preferably all four):

American-English Usage (Oxford University Press). This is the classic guide to proper usage and meanings of common terms in the English language as Americans speak it.

The Elements of Style (Macmillan). This little eighty-five-page treasure is the most concise directory to common problems in

English language usage ever published. Originally written by William Strunk, (an English teacher whose constant cry was "Omit needless words!"), the latest edition was revised by Strunk's admiring student, American writer E. B. White. Available in paperback.

Modern American Usage (Hill and Wang). Contains many terms covered in *American-English Usage* and is a good guide to punctuation. Available in paperback.

A Writer's Guide (Prentice-Hall). Explains all the concepts of grammar clearly and logically, with helpful tips on spelling.

4. An almanac, such as:

Information Please Almanac (Simon and Schuster). This annual is a valuable chronology of the year's events. Sports records, literary, film, and theatrical awards are included.

The World Almanac and Book of Facts (Newspaper Enterprise Association). This annual contains statistics on political, educational, financial, and religious subjects, as well as a historical list of famous events. In Nevada in 1936, the *Almanac* tells you, 31,925 people voted for President Franklin D. Roosevelt and 11,923 people voted for his opponent, Alf Landon.

5. A desk encyclopedia, such as:

The New Columbia Encyclopedia (Columbia University Press). Well-illustrated, ready reference covering the arts and literature, geopraphy, and physical and social sciences.

6. A gazeteer, such as:

Columbia Lippincott Gazeteer of the World (Columbia University Press). Alphabetizes and locates the places of the world, including spellings, geographical locations, trade, and natural resources.

Webster's New Geographical Dictionary (Merriam). Lists geographical names, including historical names, from Biblical times. Gives locations and population.

7. A telephone book.

THREE WAYS TO DEVELOP
THE MAGAZINE ARTICLE

Like all writing, magazine articles can be developed three ways: using exposition, narration, or persuasion. None of these categories is exclusive, and an article can be both expository and persuasive, for example, but most articles will usually emphasize one approach over another. Before you begin your article, you should understand the differences.

Exposition explains, narration tells a story, and persuasion presents an argument. A how-to article is expository, a personal experience is narrative, and a point-of-view is persuasive. (See Chapter Three for an explanation of article types.)

Exposition. Statistics, facts, even diagrams add authority to an expository article. If you are writing an article on how to lift weights, you should include an explanation of what constitutes a set of weights, how much a set costs, how to judge how much weight to lift each day to avoid injury, how much girth you can expect to add, perhaps even a diagram of various lifts to use for different results.

If you are not a weightlifter, or even if you are, you will have to gather the parts of information you do not have. List where you will check to learn what you need to know. If you decide on photographs, arrange for a photographer. (To learn whether you need one, see Chapter Nine.) Expository articles usually combine library research, phone inquiries, and interviews. Allow enough time to finish all these tasks.

Narration. The central figure in a narration is the storyteller. You may be telling the story, but more often you will be interviewing someone with a story to tell. Plan more than one interview session. The return is for afterthoughts and corrections to the original story, usually improvements. Interviewees (not to mention interviewers) also tire after more than two hours, so a second session will be more productive than one long session.

© 1974 United Feature Syndicate, Inc.

Quotes lift narration; they are its central element. As you interview, note with an asterisk (*) particularly exciting or revealing comments. You may gather your first or last paragraph from these quotes.

If you want photographs, schedule a separate session for photography or bring the photographer with you the second time. The subject will be more relaxed, and so will you.

Persuasion. To persuade successfully, an article must be thoroughly documented. An argument with out-of-date facts is usually fallacious. As you might guess, preparing this type of article sends you directly to the library, not only for information on your subject, but also for examples of successful writers of persuasion—Mary McGrory, Walter Lippmann, H. L. Mencken, or William F. Buckley, perhaps.

Persuasive articles, more than narration or exposition, take time. Allow at least six weeks for research and interviews. Write your first draft at least two weeks before the article is due to allow for extensive rewriting and polishing. Photographs are rarely necessary, which saves more time for research.

HOW TO BEGIN RESEARCH

Decide first which approach you will take with your article—will you inform, tell a story, or persuade? Check your subject in the encyclopedia, then in your telephone book. Surprising sources of information can be found in both places.

Begin your telephone contacts. Sometimes this will mean a second contact with someone you used as a source of information for your query, to let the person know you have a go-ahead from your editor. List on a tablet all the people you call, with their phone numbers, to avoid retrieving little slips of paper from pockets, bulletin boards, and garbage cans. This is your contact list, which you should keep in your research file.

Learn to ask specific questions when you use the telephone for preliminary inquiries. Speak slowly, even write out your questions before you start. To elicit specific answers, ask specific questions. For instance, contrast the following conversations.

"*Hello. General Roofing Contractors.*"

"*Hello. I'm doing an article on solar collectors. I have been asked to find out just how much it costs to fit a house with solar collectors when the house already has traditional heating equipment. I need the information for a magazine article I'm doing. I wouldn't need very much time with anybody, maybe half an hour, and I could come next Wednesday, if you're free.*"

"*Solar collectors? What magazine are you doing the article for?*"

"*Family Circle.*"

"*Oh, that's a good magazine. I read it all the time. Do you have a house that needs a new roof?*"

"*No. My roof is fine. I just need someone to talk with about solar collectors.*"

"*Oh. Well, we don't put solar collectors on roofs. We just put roofs on roofs.*"

"*Oh. Well, do you know anyone who does?*"

"*My uncle just put a solar collector on his roof for his pool, but that wasn't for his house.*"

"*What is your uncle's name?*"

"*Oh, I don't think he could help you. He lives in Florida, and we're in California.*"

"*Oh, well, thank you. Good-bye.*"

A time-saving alternative, which would have avoided confusion, is:

> *"Hello. My name is* _____. *I'm writing an article for* Family Circle *magazine to teach people how to install solar collectors on their homes. Does your company install solar collectors?"*

Remember to identify yourself, the magazine for which you are writing, and then the topic you are researching. Use the telephone efficiently.

SETTING A SCHEDULE

Once you have a list of telephone contacts, set a schedule of four to six weeks to complete your article. A sample schedule for a 1,500-word informational article with color slides you will take yourself might be:

First week. Make phone contacts and do library research (see Chapter Seven).

Second week. Do interviews (see Chapter Eight.) Arrange the first photographic session.

Third week. Write first draft (see Chapter Ten). Recheck and verify any loose material. Put your manuscript away for at least three days. Examine slides and arrange second photo session, if possible.

Fourth week. Retrieve the manuscript. Rewrite, edit mercilessly, (see Chapter Twelve) and mail the manuscript with the photographs.

This schedule can be expanded to allow a week more for research or for interviews. Putting away your manuscript allows you to edit with malice and detachment, which makes a better article.

If you are taking black-and-white photographs, allow at least three weeks from the date you plan to take the pictures for correct film processing and printing. Allow enough time to complete two photo sessions (see Chapter Nine). A one-time event does not offer this luxury. If you must hire a photographer, allow time to find one.

An approximate schedule should be four weeks for a 1,500-word article with no photographs or with color slides and six weeks for a 1,500-word article with black-and-white photography or where you must hire a photographer. Allow more time if your article requires travel, exceptional research, or unusual photography, but try to finish within two months or your editor may lose interest.

THE RESPONSE LETTER

As soon as you establish a schedule, write a response letter to your editor setting a reachable deadline for you to mail the manuscript.

A response letter simply acknowledges the editor's interest and tells him or her when you expect to complete the article. This is a courtesy, but the letter also is a reminder that you have an article working so the editor does not reassign the same idea to someone else. (No need to enclose an SASE.)

Now that you are organized, the schedule begins—so why aren't you in the library?

FOR MORE INFORMATION

As need and money dictate, add to your home reference library. Following are some suggestions.

1. An atlas, such as:

Goode's World Atlas (Rand McNally). Contains political and physical maps and resource and product maps. The United States is shown in sections, but not in states. A fine, small atlas.

Your Name
Street Address
City, State, Zip
Phone
Date

Editor's Name
Name of Publication
Street Address
City, State, Zip

Dear (Editor's Name) :

Thank you for expressing an interest in my article on Shirley Boccaccio, "San Franciscan Devoted to Role of Mother, Not Wife."

I will mail the 1,000-word article and color transparencies in one month.

Cordially,

Your Name

Hammond Medallion World Atlas (Hammond). An extensive index of names makes this a very useful tool with very legible maps. States of the United States are shown individually. Hammond makes several variations of atlases in size and price.

2. A journalism stylebook, which explains how journalistic style may differ from traditional American usage, such as:

The Associated Press Stylebook and Libel Manual (Associated Press). Originally compiled for AP's internal use, this alphabetized stylebook is a fine guide for current phrases and commonly misused or misspelled words. Handy legal reference section on libel.

A Manual of Style (University of Chicago Press). This complete stylebook is especially strong in its treatment of compound words, capitalization, and bibliographic notation.

The Washington Post Deskbook on Style (McGraw-Hill). This book, organized into chapters, devotes six chapters to language usage, but also includes ethics, fairness, taste, and typography.

3. A book of quotations, such as:

Familiar Quotations (Little, Brown). Arranged by authors chronologically. Paperback available.

The Home Book of Quotations (Dodd). More than 50,000 quotations arranged alphabetically by subject.

Peter's Quotations, Ideas for Our Time (Morrow). The author of *The Peter Principle* gathered some ancient and modern gems for contemporary readers. Indexed by subject, as well as by names and authors.

4. A biographical dictionary, such as:

Webster's Biographical Dictionary (Merriam). More than 40,000 brief, condensed biographies of noteworthy persons, with name pronunciations. You can learn, for example, that Pinckney Benton Stewart Pinchback was a nineteenth-century American politician, son of a white planter and a black slave, who was elected to the House of Representatives in 1872 and to the Senate in 1873, but was never seated.

7

Researching
Your Article

*T*he first sign of a poorly researched article is a series of generalizations. "Many people think that. . ." or "Recently, one expert theorized that. . ." indicates shoddy research. An article filled with vague references signals an article written the night before the deadline.

The key to efficient library research is knowing where an article or a statistic is most likely to be before you start wandering around the library. Therefore, you must understand how your library is organized.

The mere mention of research makes some people balk. Learning to use research tools efficiently, however, means that you can spend less time looking for something and more time enjoying what it is you want to find.

TYPES OF RESOURCES

Research information for articles basically comes from six sources.

Abstracts, dictionaries, encyclopedias, and indexes. These are your maps for information. Abstracts catalog as well as summarize each article listed. Dictionaries help you understand terminology particular to your subject, and encyclopedias are a good source of information to begin your research. Indexes are often supplemented monthly with cumulative indexes printed yearly or less often.

Books. Most books are published about a year after the completed manuscript reaches the publisher. Only a few paperback publishers work on a shorter deadline. Usually books provide the most carefully edited, verified information, but they are less timely than magazines.

Magazines. Publication deadlines for magazines run from a week (newsmagazines such as *Time* and *Newsweek*) to four months (some Sunday magazine newspaper supplements, for instance, are printed by photogravure, a complicated process that takes several weeks). The average magazine editor is thinking three or more months ahead, so as a researcher you should understand that today's magazine material is at least two or three months old. Magazines offer a more reflective overview than pamphlets and brochures.

Pamphlets and brochures. Printed for a specific purpose, topical pamphlets and brochures contain what librarians call "ephemeral" material—usually of fleeting interest and timely, but less so than newspapers.

Newspapers. The daily deadlines for "literature in a hurry" guarantee some errors. Of course, newspapers provide the most current printed information. Television and radio information may give you some leads, but printed verification of a story is more complete. Names in a newspaper story about a subject that interests you for a possible article are your lead to your first interview.

Interviews. The most timely resource of all is an interview with an expert, by telephone, letter, or in person. This process may, in turn, lead you right back to more printed material or more interviews, where the whole process begins again. (Interviews are discussed in Chapter Eight.)

LIBRARY ORGANIZATION

Finding the closest public library is easy. University and private collections often are not so visible. The *American Library Directory*, a standard reference available in almost every library, lists all libraries in the United States and Canada by state and then by city. It includes public, educational, and U.S. Armed Forces Libraries.

Each library card catalog is organized in one of two ways—using Dewey Decimal or Library of Congress classifications. Large and academic libraries favor Library of Congress; smaller libraries often use Dewey Decimal.

Dewey classifications start with three numbers; Library of Congress headings use one to three letters. The Dewey classification for American fiction, for example, is *813*, while the Library of Congress headings catalog all American literature under *PS*. Libraries usually use the card catalog to direct you to books, magazines, and newspapers, while pamphlets and brochures may be indexed separately.

GENERAL REFERENCES

Magazine writers are generalists, forced to become specialists in many fields quickly. It is surprising what you can teach yourself in the month before an article is due, but so you won't flounder for too long, here are some handy general guides to help you begin your research.

Biographical Dictionaries Master Index (1975 to date) lists more than 750,000 names of people who appear in biographical directories and tells you in which directory you can find them. Includes all the *Marquis Who's Who* publications, such as *Who's Who in America*,

Who's Who in the West, *Who Was Who*, even *Who's Who in Boxing* and *Who's Who in Jazz*. If you are doing a profile, check the name in this index, which will tell you in which biographical directory you can find information about your subject. Biographical directories are also a wonderful source for addresses of well-known people or their agents.

Facts on File (1940 to date) is a weekly, loose-leaf world news digest with a cumulative index. Covers world and national affairs, science, finance, religion, sports, and obituaries. An invaluable guide for up-to-date statistics and information.

Illustration Index (1966, supplements through 1971) tells you in what periodical you can find illustrations of just about anything you need, listed by subject. You can, for instance, learn that an illustration of bathtubs from the fourth century B. C. to the nineteenth century appeared in the February 27, 1956 issue of *Life* magazine.

Polk's Directory is an annual. Polk's publishes city directories for all major cities and some suburban areas. This is a reverse directory, so that if you have someone's address or phone number you can find out their name, how many people live at that address, and their occupations. The Polk people go door-to-door every year to solicit this information, which is not always current, but offers a beginning for hard-to-find information. Many real estate people use Polk's, as do police officers and reporters. This is a very sneaky tool, but also very helpful.

Statistical Abstract of the United States (1878 to date) summarizes statistics of the political, social, and economic organization of the United States. If you want to know the marriage or divorce rate, the birth rate, or the average temperature in a specific American city, check here. Some statistical tables go back to 1789.

Subject Guide to Books in Print, an annual, lists all the books currently being published in the United States, organized by subject. *Books in Print* lists books by subject, author, and title. *Paperback*

Books in Print does the same for paperbacks—a good starting place to learn what is being published on your topic.

HOW TO FIND BOOKS, PAMPHLETS, AND BROCHURES

Books in your library card catalog are listed alphabetically by title, author, and sometimes subject. If your library does not have a book you need, check the *Library of Congress Catalog of Printed Cards* and the *National Union Catalog,* which will tell you which libraries in the United States carry your book. Your librarian may be able to request the book for you through interlibrary loan.

The diversity and frequency of pamphlets and brochures make a national pamphlet and brochure index difficult to imagine. Libraries usually catalog pamphlets and brochures separately, so ask your librarian. Often included in these files are directories and official documents, which may be as timely as the latest Chamber of Commerce data on the average income of residents in your area or as dated as an 1880 Los Angeles real estate brochure, offering land at five dollars an acre.

HOW TO FIND MAGAZINE AND NEWSPAPER ARTICLES

Indexes to magazine articles are listed in Chapter Three under How to Do a Topic Analysis. The magazines covered are shown at the front of each index.

If you find an article in an index, but your library does not have the periodical, check the *Union List of Serials in the United States and Canada.* This directory tells you which libraries carry which magazines, complete with the dates of the magazines they carry. Your librarian can arrange for photocopies of this material for research.

Major newspapers publish their own indexes. Since 1913, the *New York Times Index* has listed, with brief summations, articles that have appeared in the *Times*, arranged by subject, with the dates they appeared. The *Times* also publishes *New York Times Film Reviews*, a collection of published reviews particularly useful for its listing of cast and credits for each film; *New York Times Theater Reviews*, also with cast and credits; and an *Obituaries Index*, useful for biographical information on prominent people.

The *Wall Street Journal* and the *London Times* each has its own index. *Newspaper Index*, published by Bell and Howell, indexes the *Chicago Tribune*, *Detroit News*, *Houston Post*, *Los Angeles Times*, *New Orleans Times-Picayune*, *San Francisco Chronicle*, and *Washington Post*.

Your library may have established its own index to articles from local newspapers. Check with your librarian. Your library also will have an index to the periodicals it carries. Many libraries leave current issues out for reading and place older issues on the shelves. Periodicals, especially those bound in yearly collections, often do not circulate, so photocopies are your only access.

MICROFILM, MICROFICHE, OR MICROCARD MATERIALS

Material that is too bulky or too precious to keep on library shelves, such as old newspapers or one-of-a-kind historical documents, is often transferred to microfilm, microfiche, or microcard. These tiny treasures must be viewed with special, but simple-to-operate, machines, and you may have printed copies made from these materials. Usually micro materials are catalogued separately, as are film strips and videotapes. Again, your librarian can direct you.

SPECIAL RESEARCH MATERIALS

Most libraries do not stock photographs or correspondence. If you are interested in this type of material, check *A Guide to Archives and Manuscripts in the United States.*

The most specific research collection is a special collection, usually devoted to one person or subject. This material can range from the Academy of Motion Picture Arts and Sciences Margaret Herrick Library collection of old movie scripts to the University of Illinois, Urbana/Champaign Mandeville Collection in Parapsychology, which includes more than 5,000 items of information about ghosts, witches, and flying saucers.

Special collections are listed in *Subject Collections.* This material is usually not available for photocopying and must be viewed at the library where the material is kept. To avoid theft, some special collection libraries allow you to bring only a pencil and paper into the room. Others may require special permission for access to their materials, so check with the librarian listed in the *Subject Collections* directory before you go.

PHOTOCOPYING FOR RESEARCH

The Copyright Act of 1976 allows you or a librarian to make one photocopy of material that you plan to use for research. Making twenty copies of an article to share with friends is considered "systematic" photocopying, which is a violation of the Copyright Act. For legal limits on fair use (how much material you may use in your article from someone else's writing) see Chapter Eleven.

FREEDOM OF INFORMATION ACT

Many states have enacted freedom of information and open meetings legislation, which gives a writer better access to public documents and public information. If you plan to write about government, check your state's position on open records and open meetings.

The 1966 federal Freedom of Information Act was amended substantially in 1974. The three major provisions of the Act provide that:

1. Every agency subject to the Act must publish its address, phone, and names of executives in the *Federal Register* (to help people find who has the records they need).

2. Agencies must make available final opinions and orders (from court cases), statements of policy, and administrative staff manuals and instructions, with an index.

3. Agencies must make available upon request *reasonably described* records. This is the most important provision for writers. You must have a fairly specific idea of what it is you are seeking to meet the *reasonably described* provision.

Once you have made your request, the agency has ten working days to answer or to notify you that the request is denied, with the reason(s). You can then appeal the agency decision. Nine categories of information are excluded, such as personnel matters, records that affect the national security, or interagency letters and memorandums.

If your research requires *Freedom of Information* material, begin early and allow for delays because of refusals and appeals. Tenacity may be rewarded.

USING NOTECARDS

One good way to keep track of all this research is to use 3 x 5 notecards to list each of your resources. List the name of the publication, author, place of publication, publisher, and date of publication. For magazine articles, include the volume and number of the periodical, as well as the page numbers. Note the date and page for newspaper articles as well.

Number each of these notecards, starting with one, as you use resources. Number your notes from that article or photocopies with the same number. This saves having to write on all your notes the source of the information. And when you are finished, the notecards are easy to arrange alphabetically for a bibliography, if you should need one.

REFERENCE SOURCES
FOR COMMON SUBJECTS

On the following pages are some helpful reference sources for ten common article subjects. (Some of these sources already have been cited in Chapter Three as mailing list possibilities.)

Business and consumerism

Consumers Index (1973 to date). An annual index to books, articles, and pamphlets on particular subjects of interest to the general consumer, such as frying pans, bike carriers, and automobiles.

Standard and Poor's Register of Corporations, Directors and Executives. An annual, listing addresses and phone numbers, as well as officers, number of employees, and yearly sales figures for nearly 40,000 American corporations.

Education

Current Index to Journals in Education (1969 to date). Monthly index of articles in more than 700 education-related academic journals, with a subject and author index.

Dictionary of Education. Defines more than 30,000 terms for this jargon-prone discipline.

The Encyclopedia of Education. More than 1,000 articles dealing with the history, theory, research, and structure of education. A listing after each article refers you to further resources.

Environment

The Environment Index (1971 to date). An annual, one-volume index of books, periodicals, newspapers, reports, and statistics on the environment by subject. Also includes a report on current federal environmental legislation and a directory of pollution control officers. A companion volume is *The Energy Index*, which also indexes annually books, periodicals, newspapers, and reports, but the scope is energy users and producers.

Government and politics (national and state)

The Federal Directory. Semiannual listing of federal employees by name, address, and agency focusing on Washington, D.C., but with some regional offices and phone numbers.

Monthly Catalog of United States Government Publications. Monthly with an annual index. You can learn what the government currently is publishing on just about any topic.

Public Affairs Information Service Bulletin. Annual, includes books and magazines, as well as pamphlets and documents that discuss issues in economics, international affairs, and political science.

Taylor's Encyclopedia of Government Officials. Monthly update (loose-leaf) makes this the most current listing of federal and state officials. Also includes a political crossword puzzle to distract you from the research you should be doing.

Home and hobbies

Index to Handicrafts, Model Making and Workshop Projects (Updated with supplements through 1973). An index to books and periodical articles on home and craft projects, from "abacus" through "jigsaws" to "yarn toys." According to the authors, none of these magazines is listed in *Reader's Guide.*

Practical Encyclopedia of Crafts. Step-by-step instructions on how to use papier mâché, for example, or how to cut gemstones, with illustrations.

Reader's Digest Complete Do-It-Yourself Manual. Comprehensive guide to home-related repairs—how to unclog your drainpipe as well as how to make aluminum storm windows.

International affairs

Dictionary of Foreign Phrases and Abbreviations by Kevin Guinagh. Common phrases in French, German, Greek, Hebrew, Irish, Italian, Latin, Portuguese, and Spanish translated into English. "Que m'aime, aime mon chien" is French for "Love me, love my dog."

Europa Year Book. Annual in two volumes. Most comprehensive of all international statistical and political information directories. Volume I covers Europe and Volume II lists the rest of the countries of the world. Includes publishers, newspapers, radio, and TV stations in each country.

Statesman's Yearbook. In addition to traditional information about who governs a country, details in one volume current welfare benefits, tourism, crime statistics, and energy and natural resources available. Valuable annual list of reference books for each country.

Statistical Yearbook, United Nations Statistical Office. Annual with population, agriculture, mining, manufacturing, trade, and social statistics for U. N. countries.

Law

Index to Legal Periodicals (1908 to date). Organized by subject and author. You can find "Tax Frauds and the Government's Right to Access to Taxpayer's Books and Records" by R.K. Van Wert in the *Pepperdine Law Review,* Spring 1978.

Cluing Into Legal Research by Peter Jan Honigsberg. Layperson's approach to how and where to find legal materials—"A Simple Guide to Finding the Law."

The Complete Layman's Guide to the Law by John Hanna. A

practical handbook of legal advice, from auto accidents to real estate.

Law and the Courts. A handy paperback guide to court structure, available by mail from the American Bar Association, Circulation Dept. 4030, 1155 East 60th Street, Chicago, Illinois 60637.

Science, medicine, and technology

How It Works. An illustrated encyclopedia of science and technology with color photographs and simplified descriptions of technical topics in twenty-two volumes, with glossary. You can learn how an airport is organized, for instance, or what the "AM" in AM radio represents.

Index Medicus (1960 to date). A monthly bibliography of academic medical literature for physicians, but a worthwhile source to spot new trends in research. Organized by author and subject.

Psychological Abstracts (1927 to date). A monthly bibliography of new books, journal articles, technical reports, and other scientific documents, with a brief discussion of each item. Indexed by author and subject.

Sports and outdoor recreation

Outdoor Recreation by Robert G. Schipf. A guide to books and periodicals on everything from *Touring the Old West* to *Short Walks in Connecticut, Volume 3.* Intended for librarians, but a quick reference tool for information on outdoor trips and hobbies.

Sports by Marshall E. Nunn. Describes 649 books on American sports, as well as ninety-three sports periodicals arranged by subject, with a list of associations and publishers.

Travel

Hotel and Travel Index, quarterly; the paperback guide a travel agent uses. Worldwide travel information on hotels and room rates from Abu Dhabi to Zimbabwe. This is the shorter version of *The Official Hotel and Travel Guide*, loose-leaf, in three volumes.

Travel Research Bibliography by the Travel Reference Center. Extensive listing of books on travel in five sections: (1) periodicals and reports, (2) bibliographies, (3) national items dealing with travel in the United States, (4) state publications (dealing with travel within the United States) and (5) international publications. Uses a subject index.

FOR MORE INFORMATION

Of course, there are reference books on reference books. *Guide to Reference Books* reviews and catalogs reference books, published in 1976 with a 1980 supplement. *American Reference Books Annual* (1970 to date) is an index of reference books with author-subject-title index.

The federal government publishes a comprehensive collection on the Freedom of Information Act, entitled *Freedom of Information Act Source Book: Legislative Materials, Cases, Articles*, available from the U.S. Government Printing Office, Washington, D. C. 20402.

8

How to Interview

A beginning interviewer's typical worry is that the interviewee will not want to be interviewed. Movie portrayals of ragged journalists chasing reluctant government officials and film stars can distort your perception of the interview's purpose and pace.

Rarely is the magazine writer faced with an unfriendly interviewee snarling "no comment." Journalist A. J. Liebling wrote in the *New Yorker:* "There is almost no circumstance under which an American doesn't like to be interviewed. . . . We are an articulate people, pleased by attention, covetous of being singled out."

An interview can be as simple as a telephone inquiry for a single piece of information ("How long has she served as governor?") or as complicated as a detailed examination with an expert of why people suffer from insomnia.

Inquiries are short and the information quickly available. By contrast, interviews take time, preparation, and imagination. Save formal interviews for your last research effort and look for information elsewhere before organizing a formal interview.

An administrative assistant, for example, can often provide factual information on current state legislation on an issue, which saves an interview with the legislator. A research assistant can send you industry and real estate statistics, which saves you an interview with the director of the Chamber of Commerce. Formal interviews should be saved for people who can give you anecdotes or perspective you can find nowhere else.

FORMS OF INTERVIEWS

The five forms of interviews are:

Factual interview. Your interviewee has technical information on a process, a machine, or a discovery that needs explanation. "What process does this equipment use to make seaweed taste like hamburger?"

Personality interview. Your interview must reveal the idiosyncrasies, habits, surroundings, and appearance, as well as the comments of the interviewee. "Describe for me what it was like living in Beverly Hills in the 1940s," you ask, noting the broken window, the mangy cat loping across the soiled linoleum floor, and the unraveling hemline on her thin cotton dress.

Narrative interview. Your interviewee's experiences will form the focus of your article. "Tell me, when the boat capsized and you saw the Coast Guard turn away from where you were in the water, did you give up?"

Interpretative interview. Your interviewee is in a position to hold a legitimate opinion on an issue you are investigating. "In your opinion, why should the government subsidize 400,000 windmills to improve our energy supply?"

Investigative interview. Your interviewee knows information that will expose someone else. "Tell me, how did you trace the illegal campaign contributions to the attorney general's bank account?"

The interview begins when you make the first phone call asking for an appointment and ends only when the article is in print. From first to last, the way you handle the people you contact will be as important as the questions you ask them, and both will determine the quality of the answers you receive.

YOUR FIRST CONTACT

When you telephone to set up an interview appointment, first identify yourself, then the magazine for which you are writing the article, then the reason you feel this person is the only one who can help you. Always be polite and cordial. For example: "Hello, Mr. Smithers, I'm _____. I've been asked by _____ magazine to do an article on Dr. Morgan Fielding's experiments with executives who use his method to lower their blood pressure through exercise and diet. Because you were one of his patients, he suggested you might be willing to talk with me."

This series of facts legitimizes you with the interviewee. Your name may mean little, but perhaps Fielding mentioned to Smithers that someone was doing an article on the topic. Next, the name of the magazine may be familiar, which verifies your purpose further. And, finally, knowing enough to single out this successful patient on Fielding's recommendation makes you even more believable. Your interviewee's answer should be "Yes."

If Smithers has a secretary, do not try to explain your project in detail. Give just your name, the magazine, and your topic, and tell the secretary you would like to talk to Smithers. If the secretary says he is not in, ask when he will return and leave a message. If Smithers does not return your call, call back. After a few tries, call Smithers at lunchtime when his secretary may be away (perhaps he sometimes eats at his desk and answers his own phone) or call him at home in the evening. Persistence pays.

Whether what you need is a telephone or a personal interview, once Smithers has consented to talk to you, ask him when you can call back or visit him to ask some questions on the subject. If he says, "Well, right now is fine," cordially decline and ask to do the interview in a couple of days.

This delay gives Smithers time to collect his ideas, maybe even some important personal statistics from the experiment. You can suggest some areas he should be thinking about ("You might try to remember which part of the exercise or diet program was the most difficult for you and how you have changed your daily routine as a result"). Then ask Smithers if there are resources you can read to further familiarize yourself with the subject. All of this improves your prospects for a good interview.

Tell your interviewee how much time you will need and ask when would be most convenient. Half an hour is probably a maximum for a phone interview. For personal interviews, suggest an hour, even though you will probably take longer. To suggest more time might scare away the subject. Schedule at least two hours between your interviews to avoid having to leave abruptly before you feel the interview is concluded. Also, try to interview your subject away from the normal office setting. Question a university scientist in the cafeteria or an executive at home. If you suggest lunch or coffee, you pay the bill (and save the receipt— see Appendix A).

PREPARING FOR THE INTERVIEW

Researching the subject, of course, is crucial. This helps you "triangulate"—test two pieces of information against a third— during the interview. Executives, public officials, and prominent personalities usually have biographies ready for the asking or are listed in standard biographical indexes (see Chapter Seven).

Always ask for biographical information ahead of time, preferably from a secretary. Never go into an interview and ask for this preliminary information, which flags you as unprepared and disorganized. The correct spelling of someone's name is an essential piece of information, but not one you need to ask in an interview. If your interviewee or your topic is controversial, talk to the adversaries beforehand for questions you can use to challenge your subject.

Prepare a list of ten questions you would like your interviewee to answer. The first question you ask is the most important because it sets the tone and indicates how prepared you are. Avoid questions that can be answered "Yes" or "No" because they do not promote conversation. Instead ask "How do you feel about . . .?" or "Can you describe for me . . .?"

Questions from your list can fill lulls in the conversation, but you should also check this list before you leave the interview to make sure you have not overlooked a point you felt was important.

FRIENDLY AND UNFRIENDLY INTERVIEWS

Interviews can be divided into "friendly" and "unfriendly." Ninety percent of a magazine writer's interviewees are friendly, which means sympathetic and helpful, with nothing to hide.

In unfriendly interviews, save difficult questions for the end. If you ask sensitive questions at the beginning, angering your subject, the interview may end abruptly almost before it starts, or the subject may grow tense, which affects the rest of the answers.

For the unfriendly interview, writer Jessica Mitford offers an interesting approach. In her book *Poison Penmanship*, she writes:

> . . . I list the questions in graduated form from Kind to Cruel. Kind questions are designed to lull your quarry into a conversational mood: "How did you first get interested in funeral directing as a career?" "Could you

suggest any reading material that might help me to understand more about problems of (the Department of) Corrections?" and so on. By the time you get to the Cruel questions—"What is the wholesale cost of your casket retailing for three thousand dollars?" "How do you justify censoring a prisoner's correspondence with his lawyer in violation of California law?"—your interlocutor will find it hard to duck and may blurt out a quotable nugget.[1]

TAKING NOTES

A stenographer's notebook and three felt-tipped pens are all you need to take notes. In Great Britain, journalists are required to study shorthand; you may find a shorthand class available through high school evening classes. If so, it is worth your time.

American journalists sometimes know shorthand, but more often struggle with their own form of quick writing, using abbreviations and acronyms to speed the process. "He worked for the railroad for four years" becomes "wrkd 4 RR 4 yrs." You can devise your own system.

Tape recorders offer an attractive alternative to the traditional notepad. Some journalists, however call tape recorders "two-pound pencils" because the machines can be intrusive, inhibiting, and cumbersome. Like many mechanical shortcuts, tape recorders have their disadvantages.

Most public people do not mind tape recorders; in fact, they often welcome them to avoid misquoting. People who are unaccustomed to being interviewed, however, may shy away from having their every word etched on tape.

If possible, carry your tape recorder in a briefcase, loaded with a tape that runs an hour on a side to avoid having to change the tape often. Once you are seated and about to begin, ask permission to use the recorder if you feel the subject will not be inhibited.

[1]Jessica Mitford, *Poison Penmanship: The Gentle Art of Muckraking* (New York: Knopf, 1979).

Always ask permission first and then assemble the equipment with minimum disruption.

One writer spent two days transcribing the tape recording of a senior government official who sounded like Mickey Mouse because she had relied on portable recorder batteries to tape the conversation. Tapes can also slip, break, or fail to run at all. To avoid these hazards, always plug in your tape recorder, check it often to make sure the tape is turning, and TAKE NOTES ANYWAY.

If this is your first interview, practice on friends and family. To help speed up your notetaking skills, turn on the radio and take notes, trying to keep up with the pace of conversation, and then transcribe your notes. You can even practice outloud the questions you plan to ask, checking for succinctness.

THE DAY OF THE INTERVIEW

Arrive on time for the interview, dressed modestly and neatly. Your purpose is not to bring attention to yourself, but to focus attention on the interviewee. Showy, flamboyant manners or clothing can only detract from this purpose. Before you enter the room where you are going to do the interview, take a deep breath, a relaxing device borrowed from the theatre. Do not use your subject's first name until he or she tells you it is acceptable. Act professional, even if your stomach flutters.

This excerpt from the play "Mark Twain Tonight!" is an example of how a wily interviewee can thoroughly befuddle an inexperienced interviewer. This incident begins with the elderly Mark Twain (played by Hal Holbrook) speaking.

> When I got back to San Francisco I found myself out of a job—so I hired a hall and gave a lecture. I've never had to do a day's work since. I had a new career. I went forth upon the public highway, with all the other bandits, and gave readings from my works. I made the acquaintance of that constant

menace to the itinerant lecturer, the local interviewer. It is petrified custom with these people to probe you with personal questions which you try to answer as conscientiously as you can; then they run home and improve you. The result is that you do not recognize yourself in print, unless you happen to be an idiot of long standing, with no prejudices about it.

For years I have tried to outwit these people. One of those villains came to me one day, when I was out on a raid. He knocked on my hotel room door and announced that he was connected with the Daily Thunderstorm. I was going to break the chair over him, but he sat down on it before I could go into action. I was not at my best that morning. My powers were somewhat under a cloud. So I decided that I had better try to confuse him.

He started it off. He said, "You know it is the custom, now, to interview any man who has become notorious."

"What do you do it with?"

"Ah, well, customarily it consists in the interviewer asking questions and the interviewed answering them. It is all the rage now. Will you let me ask you certain questions calculated to bring out the salient points of your public and private life?"

"I have a very bad memory. . ."

"Oh, that's all right. Just so you will try to do the best you can."

"I will. I will put my whole mind to it."

"Thanks. Now. Are you ready to begin?"

"Ready."

"How old are you?"

"Nineteen, in June."

"Well–I would have taken you to be much older than that."

"Thank you very much."

"Where were you born?"

"In Missouri."

"When did you first begin to write?"

"In 1836."

"Why, how could that be, if you are only nineteen now?"

"I don't know. That does strike you as curious, somehow, doesn't it?"

"Yes. Whom do you consider the most remarkable man you ever met?"

"Aaron Burr." [*]

"Aaron Burr! But you never could have met Aaron Burr if you are only nineteen years–"

"Now, if you know more about me than I do, what do you ask me for?"

"Well . . . it was only a suggestion. How did you happen to meet Burr?"

"I happened to be at his funeral one day, and he asked me to make less noise. . ."

"Good heavens! If you were at his funeral, he must have been dead; and if he was dead, how could he care whether you made a noise or not?"

"Oh, he was always a particular kind of a man that way."

"Now let me get this straight: you say he spoke to you, and yet he was dead."

"I didn't say he was dead."

"But . . . wasn't he?"

"Some said he was, some said he wasn't."

"What did you think?"

"It was none of my business. It wasn't my funeral."

"Well, let's drop that. Let me ask about something else. Have you any brothers or sisters?"

"I–I–I–think so–yes–but I don't remember."

"Well, that is the most extraordinary statement I ever heard! I'm sure you had a brother. Haven't I read that somewhere?"

"Oh. Yes, now that you mention it: there was a brother William–Bill we called him. Poor old Bill!"

"Why? Is he dead?"

"We never could tell. There was a great mystery about that, you see."

"That is sad. He disappeared, then?"

"Well, yes, in a sort of general way. We buried him."

"Buried him! Without knowing whether he was dead or not?"

"Oh, no. He was dead enough, all right. You see, we were twins–defunct and I–and we got mixed in the bathtub when we were only two weeks old, and one of us was drowned. But we didn't know which. Some think it was Bill. Some think it was me."

* *Author's note:* Aaron Burr died in 1836.

"What do you think?"

"I would give worlds to know. This solemn, this awful mystery has cast a gloom over my whole life. But I'll tell you a secret which I've never revealed to anyone before. One of us has a peculiar mark—a large mole on the back of his left hand; that was me. That child was the one that was drowned."

Then the young man withdrew.[2]

An interviewer is like a bus driver on the outside lane of a narrow mountain road. You must gingerly guide the bus wheels away from the edge of the road, always remembering your destination.

The interviewee may be as nervous as you about this experience. To give the interviewee time to evaluate you and relax, look around the room for subjects to start small talk—a smashed tennis racket in a frame hanging behind an executive, a trophy to his temper; a slot machine in a police officer's living room; green flasks in a chemist's office marked "beer" and "scotch." During this time, try to move your interviewee away from his or her desk, if you must do the interview in an office. This puts you on a more informal basis. According to *Washington Post* reporter Sally Quinn, in *(More)* magazine:

> *If you are going to get people to open up and to be themselves and to reveal something to you, I think that the best way to do it is to create an atmosphere of sympathy . . . to make that person believe or feel that you like him or her, that you can understand the fears and hopes and dreams and whatever else there is about that person.*

Begin the formal interview with the first question from your list, which should be your best question, but not combative. The interviewee will use this question to evaluate your experience, your knowledge. Make this a good beginning.

If your interviewee rambles, use the time to phrase your next question and to note mannerisms, physical characteristics, and room furnishings. Interrupt an answer only to return your inter-

---

[2]Reprinted with permission from *Mark Twain Tonight* by Hal Holbrook, copyright 1959. Published by David McKay Co., Inc. Adaptation of "Encounter with an Interviewer" from *Tom Sawyer* by Mark Twain. Harper & Row, Publishers, Inc.

viewee to the topic; you are talking too much if you are talking more than twenty-five percent of the time.

Tips for the Interviewer

1. Do not rely on an interview for statistics or dates. Your interviewee may say, "About four years ago, I. . ." Note this estimate, and if the date is important, ask for a specific date at the end of the interview; then separately verify the information through research.

2. Hide your surprise at revealing information or circumstances that add to your article. One reporter doing a profile on a notable rock music attorney walked into his office to find him in a gold hot tub with his girlfriend. They conducted the interview from there.

3. Keep off-the-record comments off-the-record. This situation usually occurs only with public officials and controversial issues. To avoid confusion, some writers feel the subject should understand at the outset that all material is on the record once the interview begins. If you accept off-the-record material, note in the margin those parts of the conversation that are confidential. Some reporters burn off-the-record notes, or erase those portions of the tape. You can also ask the subject to push the "stop" button on the recorder when he or she wishes confidentiality. This rare situation must be handled differently in each circumstance, depending upon how willing you are to give up attributed information.

4. If you do not understand something, stop the interview to ask for clarification. Do not be intimidated. "Are you saying that. . .?" is a good way to check your perception, or quoting back to the person your notes on what he or she said. Clarify any jargon or acronyms you do not understand as you go along.

5. Beware of the subject who asks *you* too many questions, such as "What do *you* think?" The subject may be evading you.

6. Beware of the word *frankly* when used by your interviewee, which usually indicates a habit and does not precede any big revelation.

7. Do not ask leading questions, such as "When did you stop beating your wife?" Answers will be understandably defensive. "Would you say that. . .?" is a good clarifier.

8. Challenge your interviewee by saying "Some critics say that. . ." or "Your opponent has called you a _____. What is your response to this criticism?" This approach deflects responsibility for the critical comments from you. "Let me play the devil's advocate" is also a good device for argumentative questions.

9. Take the issue from the general to the specific. Large issues, such as welfare or crime, overwhelm an interviewer. Be wary of government officials or business executives who speak to you in "programtalk," which is "Our program services 800,000 people" or "Our program is budgeted for $6,000,000." Personalize this and ask questions that will show how large decisions affect one individual. "What will this $6,000,000 increase in welfare benefits mean for a welfare mother of four?" is a better question than "Can you explain your new $6,000,000 benefit program?"

10. If the interviewee does not want to answer a question, point out that you will be forced to use the opposition viewpoint with no counterargument. This usually works.

11. Use your ignorance wisely. A vulnerable interviewer who says, "Can you explain this to me?" is an irresistible student.

12. Sharing experiences often elicits similar confidences from your interviewee. Use this tactic selectively, or your interviewee will be interviewing you.

13. Ask difficult questions twice, rephrasing the second time. Changing the question from the specific to the general helps. "Did you see the treasurer deposit company funds in his personal bank account?" can become "How do you feel about the ethics of an executive, such as a treasurer, who uses company funds for personal expenses?"

14. Remember the importance of follow-up questions. A

public official might be asked at a press conference if he or she paid any state income tax in the last year. The follow-up question is "Well, don't you have to sign your income tax return?" Such a follow-up corners the subject. This is an example of triangulation—using two pieces of information to elicit a third.

15. When you are probing with sensitive questions, wait a few moments after the interviewee has completed the answer. Often afterthoughts will be your best material.

Unless the interviewee stops the interview first (with such subtle tactics as handing you your tape recorder and asking you to wait outside while he or she eats lunch), the interview is over when the interviewee starts to fidget and the answers begin to repeat themselves. To signal that you are about to end, you can say, "One last question, Mr./Mrs./Miss/Ms. _____."

Leaf through your notepad to make sure you have answers to your prepared questions and to verify any statistics or dates you feel essential. Then conclude with "Is there anything else important you feel I've overlooked?" An experienced but polite interviewee may wait for this question to give you some helpful hints.

HOW TO HANDLE
THE QUESTION OF REVIEW

A person will usually wait until the end of an interview to ask you when the article will appear, and sometimes will ask to review your manuscript before the article is printed. A true answer to the first question is that you do not know when the article will be published, explaining that magazines are scheduled two to three months in advance. But assure your interviewee that as soon as you know you will call with the date and will send a copy of the article when it is published.

To the second question, about review, your response should be that you will smooth out the grammar to make the copy readable. Then ask permission to call back if you have additional questions or need to check facts, statistics, even methods—such as a description of a scientific experiment, a complicated medical procedure, or legal maneuver. Explain that you have a deadline, that your editor has final approval on all copy, and that you will be happy to send a copy of the article *once it is in print*. Never relinquish to the interviewee final approval on what you send your editor.

Then close your notebook, turn off and disconnect your tape recorder, but do not disconnect your mind from the subject. The interview is not yet officially concluded, and you may get a pointed comment or a funny anecdote as you are leaving. Do not rip furiously into your notebook to write it down because your subject may recant—but remember it. Also, assure your subject again that you will call back if you need to verify any information.

Transcribe your notes as soon as you can after the interview, adding personal observations and recollections. Unless your article will be strictly a manuscript of question and answer, do not bother to transcribe your entire tape. Skip to the portions of the tape that you feel are important and type out responses. Gather together any questions you may still have and make *one* phone call to your interviewee for clarification.

Assemble your notes, your research, and your interviews. Now you are ready to write.

FOR MORE INFORMATION

The Craft of Interviewing by John Brady (Random House paperback, 1977) and *Interviewing* (Prentice-Hall paperback, 1977) by Ken Metzler are two books that expand on interview techniques. Brady's book is anecdotal, based on several interviews he conducted with such writers as Rex Reed, Joseph Wambaugh, and Gay Talese. Metzler's book is aimed at journalism students trying to learn how to interview; contains a valuable bibliography.

9

The Writer-
Photographer

*T*he writer-photographer is a prized commodity, and your goal should be to become one, if you are not already. Most markets welcome photographs, so someone who can write as well as photograph can make more sales.

The first mistake a writer who wants to become a photographer can make is thinking that photography is easy because the equipment is relatively simple. An analogy would be thinking that writing is easy because you know how to use a typewriter. The equipment is not the source of your ideas, and your ability to photograph must come from your intellect, your imagination, and your experience.

To *take* photographs for publication, you will need a 35mm single-lens reflex camera (and the 50mm lens that comes with it), a 70–150mm zoom lens and a 28mm wide-angle lens. These three lenses will help you through most situations. Camera equipment can be expensive, with the cost easily surpassing $600, so think carefully about your ambitions to become a photographer.

To *sell* photographs, you will probably need at least a year's experience working with your 35mm camera, both in color and black-and-white. This is not to discourage you, but only to make you understand the obstacles.

WHEN TO HIRE A PHOTOGRAPHER

Even after a year's experience with a 35mm camera, you will still need a photographer at certain times, such as:

1. When the image you want requires sophisticated equipment, such as underwater photography, aerial photography, high speed photography (bullets going through sheetrock), or microphotography (photographing through a microscope).

2. When the event you need to photograph happens only once, with no opportunity for you to reshoot to correct errors or add to your acceptable list of photographs.

3. When you do not have access to an event, such as a presidential press conference, where a special press pass is required, or professional sporting events where you cannot get a pass to be on the field. (Police departments and military bases often sell photographs when they must restrict admittance to an area for security reasons.)

4. When the thing to be photographed is technically difficult—high speed races, for instance.

5. When the lighting situation is particularly tricky—night photography, for instance, or low light photography.

6. When what you have to say depends more than fifty percent on the photographs, which makes the photographs essential to selling the article.

PHOTOGRAPHIC SOURCES

If you decide that you will be unable to take photographs for your article, you have several photography sources to use. First, check with an area college, university, or photography school. Students often will work with you on speculation, waiting for payment just like you, when the story is accepted.

You should allocate at least one-quarter of any fee you receive for your article to pay the photographer. If the photographs are fifty percent of your story, then the photographer' share of your fee should be fifty percent.

Your local newspaper may have photo files and may be willing to sell you prints of pictures. Another choice is one of the larger photographic studios in town, which may have stock photos of locations in your area, such as a state capitol or a familiar monument. For a small charge, they will usually make a black-and-white print.

If you want a photograph of the Grand Canyon, for instance, or other travel sites, write to the tourist office at that spot. These photographs are called stock photos, and many associations, Chambers of Commerce, and tourist offices will provide what you need free of charge. (For a list of directories, see Chapter Three.)

Archives collections and special collections are another source of photographs (see Chapter Seven for listing). The University of California at Los Angeles, for example, holds the newspaper negatives from several early Los Angeles newspapers (including photographs of many 1930s Hollywood stars), which they will duplicate for a nominal fee.

Your last resort should be a photographic agency. These are listed in Magazine Industry Market Place under Stock Photos. Often this is an expensive choice. MIMP also lists photographers for hire. You can expect to pay $200 to $500 a day for a professional photographer's services, plus the cost of making the prints.

IF YOU ARE THE PHOTOGRAPHER

If you feel that you have enough experience and are comfortable with the situation you must photograph, check the market listing first to know whether your market requires black-and-white or color. Magazines use both color transparencies (35mm slides) and 8" x 10" black-and-white glossies. A film marked ASA 64 is good for color work; for black-and-white, ASA 125 is good for daylight and ASA 400 for dark situations.

COMMON PHOTOGRAPHIC PROBLEMS

Here are some common problems photographers face, with corrections. See if you can recognize familiar situations.

As a writer-photographer, you should be a writer first. Your first visit to your subject should be as interviewer. This will relax your subject and make your photo session easier. Unless you have no choice and must do the photographs at the same time as the interview, schedule a second session for photography. Your subject will be more relaxed, and so will you.

At the photography session, prepare your subject for a return (third) visit. You may not need one, but if you do, the visit is no embarrassment to either of you and removes from the subject's mind the idea that you are not a good enough photographer to take acceptable photos the first time.

If you can do two photographic sessions, you should, preferably at a different time of day to photograph your subject in different lighting. Outside light is, of course, best in early morning or late afternoon. Try to avoid high noon photo sessions.

Listen while you photograph. Your interviewee may clarify or enhance your first interview, especially if what you are photographing is a how-to and you must photograph each step. Keep a notepad near and tune in your memory.

Photographs 1 and 2 *Both these photographs are acceptable; however, the second one involves the viewer more intimately with the subject. A photographer who is not afraid to move closer to the subject will take photographs that are more personal.*

MODEL RELEASE

A photographer working for a publication should be familiar with a model release form. News photography does not require a release, but most magazine photography does. Be sure your subject understands and signs three copies of the model release—one for the model, one for you, and one for the magazine. Send a copy to the magazine and keep the original for your files. If the person photographed is a minor, you must have a responsible adult's permission (see Sample Model Release).

Sample Model Release

For value received, I, _(name of subject)_, hereby authorize _(name of photographer)_ to use my photograph for sale or reproduction in any medium the photographer chooses for editorial, display, exhibition, or advertising use.

I am eighteen years of age or older.

Date: Signed:

Witnessed by:

For a minor, change the form to:

For value received, I, _(name of guardian or parent)_, hereby authorize _(name of photographer)_ to use the photograph of my child(ren) _(name/s of children)_, for sale or reproduction in any medium the photographer chooses for editorial, display, exhibition, or advertising use.

I have legal right to give such consent.

Date: Signed:

Witnessed by:

EDITING PHOTOGRAPHS

You should take a ratio of four-to-one photographs to finished product—two to three rolls of 36 exposure film for twenty final images. Use the same ratio for the number of photographs you send—if the article requires five photographs, send twenty. This four-to-one ratio offers your editor choices, but not confusion.

Editing photographs is difficult. You can easily become emotionally attached to photos because they are tangible reminders of people and experiences. The photograph may be a little out-of-focus and a little dark, you reason, but this was the one perfect dive. Perfect dive or not, do not send the photograph. Good magazines will not print technically imperfect shots, so take plenty of photographs for a better choice.

Photographs 3 and 4 *The attraction of the subject in these photographs is the interaction of horizontal and vertical lines. Sometimes the photographer can become so involved in the subject that he or she overlooks distracting details in front of the subject—in this case, the No Parking sign. Also, annoying objects, such as the pole in the middle of the first photograph, cannot be removed, but by moving to the right, the photographer was able to improve the image.*

Photographs 5 and 6 *To improve a distracting background, sometimes the photographer and the subject can more over to a more neutral spot.*

Photographs 7 and 8
*Because the camera is by nature
horizontal, many photographers
forget to pay attention to a subject
and setting that dictate a vertical
photograph.*

Photographs 9 and 10 *The photographer should check the entire viewfinder, especially the edges, before taking the photograph. In this case, the rusty cyclone fence ruins the scene's picturesque quality.*

Photograph 11 *To avoid a blurred photograph, brace your elbows next to your body to keep your hand as steady as possible, and be sure your shutter speed matches the situation.*

Photographs 12 and 13 *When your subject is in uneven lighting, you can lose important facial details. If possible, move your subjects into full shade.*

HOW TO MAIL PHOTOGRAPHS

Color transparencies can be processed within twenty-four hours without a premium cost, and color is best left to a professional custom laboratory. For black-and-white, request a proof sheet first. The cost is minimal (about $3), and once you see your work you can choose which photographs to print in the more expensive 8" x 10" size. Black-and-white glossies take a week to ten days, so unless you have your own darkroom, allow three weeks of photography time if your magazine wants black-and-white—ten days for first processing and ten days in case the first set of photographs does not satisfy you and you have to do a second session.

To label color transparencies, use small name stickers in the margin of the mount. Pencil consecutive numbers on the mounts and put them into a plastic sheet holder for twenty slides, in the order you want the editor to view them. The editor can see the slides without removing them from the plastic sheet by placing them on a light table.

If you are sending black-and-white, mark numbers and your name and address in pencil on the back of each photo (or you can use a rubber stamp for your name and address). Do not use a felt tip pen, which can smear.

Type a shot list, which shows each photograph by number with a caption, or type a caption on a 10" x 2" piece of white paper and tape it to the back of each photograph (on the bottom) with masking tape. This makes your caption a flap that you can easily fold backward for shipping.

Remember that photographs should complement an article and improve the writing product. Give your editor a complete word and photographic package, where each element enhances the other. What could be more salable?

FOR MORE INFORMATION

Writing a chapter on photography is like summarizing American literature in one paragraph—too much to cover in too little space.

However, three good articles are: "Writer With a Camera" by Rus Arnold in the *Writer's Market* (1974); "Five Easy Features" by Richard Wolters in *Writer's Digest* (June 1976); and "Photography, the Law and the Writer" by Richard H. Logan III in the book *Law and the Writer* (Writer's Digest 1978).

The 17-volume *Life Library of Photography* is a very good resource on everything from travel photography to photographing children. *Photography* by Phil Davis (William C. Brown 1979, third edition) is an excellent how-to, and the current edition of *Photographer's Market* (published by the *Writer's Market* people) details more markets for your photographs.

10

Writing Your First Draft

The magazine article is a hybrid. Like the essay and the news story, an article teaches or entertains. Yet the magazine article is longer than a news story and shorter than an essay. Articles leave little room for lengthy quotations, like those in an essay, but often depend on shorter quotations to pep them up, like a news story. And like both the news story and the essay, an article must be topical.

KNOWING YOUR AUDIENCE

If you have ever given a speech, you realize the importance of defining who will be listening. A story on the "eensy weensy spider" is too young for teenagers, just as an article on the gross national product would probably not entertain five-year-olds. As a writer, you must define your audience and then speak to it.

Circulation statistics from your magazine analysis begin to tell you about your audience. So will the description of the magazine you research from magazine marketing sources. Age, education, and income level statistics for your audience will help, if available.

Circulation figures will also tell you the interest level to expect from your audience. If the circulation is 20,000 aerospace employees, for example, and your article is about proposed legislation that would affect their working conditions and salaries, you can assume a concentrated level of interest and an understanding of aerospace jargon.

If instead, you write for a magazine with a circulation of 5,000,000 to a general audience and your article is about a new variety of tomato, you may assume only a portion of your audience will be interested. So, you should avoid any agricultural terminology without definitions because not all of your audience will understand.

Reading the magazine discloses a pattern of writing you should emulate. Are paragraphs and sentences short or long? Is the language complex or simple? Do quotations and anecdotes fili the articles, or are the articles entirely exposition? Is the first person "I" used often, or are the articles in third person? These factors all influence your approach.

When you write, speak to one reader—a composite from what you can learn about the audience. Do not write to impress with your knowledge, but to express ideas to an interested, willing reader with whom you want to share your research, your experience.

DEFINING YOUR THEME

When you write a query (as discussed in Chapter Five), you define your broad idea into a topic. That topic, or a variation you modified after research, should become your theme—the central concept on which you now base your article.

You have undoubtedly known people whose conversation cannot continue on a straight highway of thought without taking several side roads. Each time such a person reaches a key word or thought, the speaker detours the conversation to explain, and often turns to you after five minutes to ask "What was I saying?" A writer who takes too many detours will elicit the same reaction.

A theme is your central thought or your central moral. Each paragraph should be a package of thoughts, linked to the other paragraphs by a consistent theme. Each sentence should be an effort to expand or enhance that theme. Any extra words, any unnecessary thoughts that detract from your theme should be ruthlessly deleted from your article, even if the thought was your most provocative, your most creative in a decade.

POINT OF VIEW

Most articles are written from the third person point of view—he or she. Once you begin an article in the third person, do not shift to the first person. Narrative articles most often invite the first person "I" point of view. Like your theme, the point of view of your article must remain consistent throughout, or you will confuse your reader.

HOW TO ORGANIZE

Before you begin writing, make notes. Decide how you will structure your article—chronologically, geographically, statistically. Will you use descriptive passages, lengthy quotations, or detailed documentation? What crucial points must you make to support your argument? Which of your interviewees provided the best quotes? Which resources gave the best material? Gather your notes, quotes, and research before you start.

Type your first draft double-spaced with one-and-a-half inch margins to allow room for your editing. Two hundred and fifty words equal one page of pica type (ten words per line), so a 1,500-word article is only six pages.

The Elements of Style, by Strunk and White (see Chapter Six under Gathering Supplies), should be beside every writer's typewriter, next to the dictionary, to answer questions on style and punctuation. A misspelled word in a first draft generally ends up misspelled in the final copy, so use your dictionary as you go along.

New York Times columnist William Safire offers a humorous reminder for vigilant grammarians:

> Not long ago, I advertised for perverse rules of grammar, along the lines of "Remember to never split an infinitive" and "The passive voice should never be used." The notion of making a mistake while laying down rules ("Think," "We Never Make Misteaks") is highly unoriginal, and it turns out that English teachers have been circulating lists of fumblerules for years.
>
> As owner of the world's largest collection, and with thanks to scores of readers, let me pass along a bunch of these never-say-neverisms:
>
> Avoid run-on sentences they are hard to read.
>
> Don't use no double negatives.
>
> Use the semicolon properly, always use it where it is appropriate; and never where it isn't.
>
> Reserve the apostrophe for it's proper use and omit it when its not needed.
>
> Do not put statements in the negative form.
>
> Verbs has to agree with their subjects.
>
> No sentence fragments.
>
> Proofread carefully to see if you any words out.
>
> Avoid commas, that are not necessary.
>
> If you reread your work, you will find on rereading that a great deal of repetition can be avoided by rereading and editing.
>
> A writer must not shift your point of view.
>
> Eschew dialect, irregardless.
>
> And don't start a sentence with a conjunction.
>
> Don't overuse exclamation marks!!!
>
> Place pronouns as close as possible, especially in long sentences, as of 10 or more words, to their antecedents.

Hyphenate between syllables and avoid un-necessary hyphens.
Write all adverbial forms correct.
Don't use contractions in formal writing.
Writing carefully, dangling participles must be avoided.
It is incumbent on us to avoid archaisms.
If any word is improper at the end of a sentence, a linking verb is.
Steer clear of incorrect forms of verbs that have snuck in the language.
Take the bull by the hand and avoid mixed metaphors.
Avoid trendy locutions that sound flaky.
Never, ever use repetitive redundancies.
Everyone should be careful to use a singular pronoun with singular nouns in their writing.
If I've told you once, I've told you a thousand times, resist hyperbole.
Also, avoid awkward or affected alliteration.
Don't string too many prepositional phrases together unless you are walking through the valley of the shadow of death.
Always pick on the correct idiom.
"Avoid overuse of 'quotation "marks." ' "
The adverb always follows the verb.
Last but not least, avoid clichés like the plague; seek viable alternatives.[1]

HOW TO STRUCTURE
YOUR ARTICLE

Like an essay, a magazine article needs an introduction, a body, and a conclusion. In a 1,500-word article, the introduction and conclusion should be no longer than two paragraphs apiece, or approximately 500 words total. This leaves 1,000 words for the body, or explanation, of your topic.

[1]William Safire, "The Fumblerules of Grammar," *New York Times Magazine*, 4 November 1979, p. 16. © 1979 by The New York Times Company. Reprinted by permission.

The Introduction. Writing teachers often tell students that the introduction to an essay should "tell the reader what you're going to say," the body should "say it," and the conclusion should "tell the reader what you've said." For an essay this works, but for a magazine article add one element—the "lead," which might be considered the first part of the introduction.

The beginning of your article needs a lead—a "hook," a quote, a characterization, an anecdote, or an interesting fact to compel the reader (and the editor) to continue reading. Your job in the introduction is to entice your audience.

If you are writing about gold, for instance, you can begin your article in one of several ways.

Fact: Twenty thousand people visit the gold country every summer, each hoping to become a modern-day prospector.

Quote: "There's more gold in these hills than anybody ever took out of them in the last hundred years of prospecting," says George "Shivers" Carver.

Characterization: "Shivers" his friends call him, because his hands shake. But the gold pan seems steady between his fingers as he reaches into the river, sifting the sand at the bottom. Shivers takes $100 worth of gold out of the river every day.

Anecdote: A hunter once wandered up to the camp where George Carver prospects every fall, randomly shooting a rifle into the bushes. After one bullet skinned a tree near Carver's head, Carver grabbed his pistol and shot. The hunter fell, his leg hit. George Carver's hands began shaking that day, fifteen years ago, and now his nickname is "Shivers." He never carried a gun again.

Each lead would be acceptable, and the publication you are writing for would determine your choice. The lead may be the theme, as in the factual example, or an attention-getting quote. Characterization and anecdote can take two paragraphs to develop, which means a slower pace for your article, but this works well for a profile.

If the lead is considered the first part of the introduction, the second part is the explanation to the reader of just where this article is going. Will you explain how to pan gold? Will you use narrative to open George Carver's personality to your reader? Or will you use your anecdote as an argument to open more national parks to gold prospectors? Your reader wants to know, and this usually means stating your theme before you finish the introduction.

The Body. As in the essay, the body of your article should explain, elaborate on your introduction. Important between paragraphs throughout your article are transitions—connections between paragraphs that carry your reader from one paragraph to another. Transition words like *but, and, yet,* and *meanwhile* continue your thoughts and the reader's. Strive for a progression of ideas from one sentence to the next, rather than introducing a new idea midparagraph, which belongs elsewhere or does not belong at all.

The Conclusion. The ending of your article should take no more than two paragraphs. Here you round up information for your reader, saying "This is where I was going. Now I'm here."

For the George Carver article, the conclusion might be a:

Fact: Of the 20,000 visitors who hike the gold country each year, ninety percent of them will see the sparkle of gold only in a jewelry store.

Quote: "I've lived here for fifteen years now," George Carver explains, "and I don't think I'll ever do anything else."

Characterization: "Shivers" crawled slowly onto his mule, kicked her sides gently, and together they loped down the hillside.

Anecdote: After some successful prospecting five years ago, Shivers bought a car and a house in town. He even got a phone and a post office box. Then people started asking him for loans, he says, so he sold the house and the car and returned to the hills. He carries $50,000 worth of gold on the side of his mule, but at least now no one is around to ask him for a loan.

Each ending is acceptable, but the approach you take throughout your article should determine your conclusion.

Following are some specific suggestions on how to handle different types of articles.

Informational. Accurate information, explained in easy language, guarantees an informational article's success. Verify and recheck every small detail.

How-to. You must be able to organize step-by-step instructions and use words that do not confuse the newcomer to the craft. If possible, duplicate the skill you are describing and watch for empty spots in your description. Think of yourself as a teacher unfolding an experiment that you expect the class to duplicate.

Profile. Profiles rely heavily on quotes, description, and your ability to interview. You must convey to your reader the presence of the person you interviewed and duplicate the feelings and emotions the person provoked in you.

Historical. Of course, dates are an important element to any historical article. Check to see that no gaps in continuity exist, that there are no unexplained missing pieces of time.

Personal experience. If the experience is your own, try to recall your feelings at each moment of the experience you are trying to recreate. If the experience is someone else's, try to duplicate the emotions of that person in your description.

Inspirational. This article's purpose is uplifting. Avoid negative thoughts and insert the feeling that hope always exists, even though hope sometimes grows out of a feeling of hopelessness or despair. The emotions of the experience are central for an inspirational article.

Humor and satire. Humor plays on imagery, word pictures, and the unexpected. One joke told quickly is not enough; the joke must build on several small jokes for effect. Transitions and timing are crucial. Read this outloud to help your pacing.

Travel. Like all descriptive writing, the travel article depends on adjectives and your ability to convey experience—what the visitor will see, hear, taste, smell, and feel. Neither the descriptions nor the locations can be cliches.

Investigative. Research, carefully cross-checked, is the foundation of the investigative article. Attribution is tricky, and the best investigations quote actual sources rather than "sources who should know." Two sources to verify an assertion may not be enough if both are unwilling to be quoted. Work to bring your subjects into the record for attribution.

Point-of-view. Think of yourself as an attorney facing a jury, with a client who is charged with murder. You must build each point to the inevitable conclusion that your client is innocent. Your point-of-view article must do the same. Transitions of thought, to keep your reader following along with your perspective, are essential.

At this point, there should be no more organizing, researching, or rearranging the pencils in your pencil holder. Set a schedule for your writing and start, even if you just type your name at the top of the page. "All writers know that on some golden mornings they are touched by the wand—are on intimate terms with poetry and cosmic truth," writes John Kenneth Galbraith. "I have experienced those moments myself. Their lesson is simple: it's a total illusion. And the danger in the illusion is that you will wait for those moments. Such is the horror of having to face the typewriter that you will spend all your time waiting."

FOR MORE INFORMATION

In this author's opinion, the best essay on writing is George Orwell's "Politics and the English Language" in his *Collection of Essays* (Harcourt, Brace 1970). Read and reread his ideas for inspiration.

Some helpful books about writing are: Thomas Elliott Berry's *The Craft of Writing* (McGraw-Hill 1974) and *The Most Common Mistakes in English Usage* (McGraw-Hill 1971); *On Writing Well* by William Zinsser (Harper 1976, second edition); and *On Writing, Editing and Publishing* by Jacques Barzun (University of Chicago Press 1971).

11

The Legalities

"*I* just write the articles. I let the magazine editors worry about the legalities," one writer said. Do not be so flippant. Copyright, fair use, libel, and right to privacy are four issues every free-lancer should understand.

COPYRIGHT RIGHTS

Copyright is a registration with the government of your rights as the creator of a work. This gives you a legal right to seek damages should unauthorized portions of your work be used without your consent or knowledge.

When you sell an article to a magazine, you relinquish whatever rights the magazine agrees to buy and you agree to sell. Your goal should be to give up the fewest rights possible, to guarantee any income you may receive from future use of the article.

Magazines usually list the rights they purchase in *Writer's Market* or other marketing aids. A statement by a magazine of rights it purchases contains three elements: (1) the priority of use for the article, (2) the country in which the article may be published, and (3) the kind of publication allowed to use the article. For example, an offer to purchase *First North American Serial Rights* (the most common) means that the magazine buys the right to print the article (1) the *first* time it will appear in (2) *North America* in a (3) *magazine* (serial is a fancy name for magazine). First European Serial Rights would mean the first time the article is published in a magazine in Europe. First World Rights would mean the first time the article appears in a magazine anywhere in the world.

Variations on this beginning might be Second American Serial Rights (the second use of the article in the United States, but not North America, which includes Canada and Mexico) or Third Central American Serial Rights (the right to use the article the third time it appears in Central America).

Rights purchased are as diverse as the markets, although specific rights sold rarely go beyond "Third," when they become "Reprint Rights," which means the right to reprint an already published work. If you sell one magazine First North American Serial rights and then sell Second North American Serial Rights to another magazine, the second magazine cannot publish your article until it is printed in the first magazine.

A writer who sells, "All Rights" has given up all claim to any income from all ways the material may be used—including second serial use, reprints, books, or films. A variation might be "All Serial Rights," which would protect book or film rights, but would give up any use of the article in a magazine. Only occasionally is the price paid for an article worth relinquishing all rights. As a rule, do not do it.

HOW TO PROTECT YOUR RIGHTS

As a writer, you have two ways to insure that you will sell only the rights you want to give up. First, on your manuscript you should type the rights available (see Chapter Twelve under Your Final Draft). This is a signal to the publication—but *not a guarantee*—that you will not be asked to sell more.

Second, when the article is accepted and the check arrives, the endorsement will usually specify which rights you are selling. Be sure you do not relinquish too many rights. If the endorsement is incorrect, do not scratch out the endorsement and write in the rights you are selling and then cash the check. Instead, return the check to the magazine and ask for a new endorsement. To avoid any misunderstandings, another approach is to ask the magazine to write you a letter, for both your signatures, stating the rights purchased and sold.

RIGHTS UNDER THE NEW COPYRIGHT ACT

In 1976, Congress passed the first omnibus revision of copyright in the United States in 1909. Provisions of the Copyright Act of 1976 cover all nonfiction copyrighted after January 1, 1978, and clarify fair use and copyright (see Fair Use—Your Right to Someone Else's Material later in this chapter). Included in the Act's protections are fiction and photography, even pantomime, choreography, sculpture, and musical works.

Compared to the 1909 Act, the 1976 Copyright Act lengthened and widened protections for authors' rights. Under the old law, copyright lasted twenty-eight years and could be renewed for twenty-eight years. The new law protects an author's copyright for his or her lifetime, plus fifty years. The old law also offered no statutory protection for unpublished works. The new law specifically provides a method for you to copyright your works, even if they are not yet published.

Most magazines published in the United States are copyrighted. If a magazine does not note its copyright in *Writer's Market* or other market publications, check a current issue of the magazine, in or near the masthead.

If a copyrighted magazine published your article, you need do no more. Your material is then protected by the magazine's copyright. If an uncopyrighted magazine publishes your article, however, you should separately register the copyright for your article with the United States Copyright Office.

HOW TO COPYRIGHT
AN UNPUBLISHED WORK

To copyright an unpublished work, request copies of Form TX and/or Form GR/CP from the Copyright Office, Library of Congress, Washington, D. C. 20559, or call the federal government information phone number for the office nearest you, and they will mail the forms.

Form TX is an Application for Copyright Registration for a Nondramatic Literary Work. According to the form, this includes "fiction, nonfiction, poetry, periodicals, textbooks, reference works, directories, catalogs, advertising copy and compilations of information (see sample forms). A page of typewritten copy qualifies as an unpublished work, but any work must be identifiable, so give your copy a title. The Copyright Office calls these "original works of authorship."

To copyright your work, send the completed form TX with one entire copy of your unpublished work or two entire copies of your published work, with a ten-dollar registration fee, to the Copyright Office.

Form GR/CP is an Adjunct Application for Copyright Registration for a Group of Contributions to Periodicals (see sample form). If you want to protect one or several articles you have written for uncopyrighted periodicals, or if you want insurance that material in a copyrighted publication is protected, send a completed Form GR/CP along with Form TX. The Adjunct Application allows you to list nineteen articles, and you can add pages for more listings.

APPLICATION FOR COPYRIGHT REGISTRATION

for a
Nondramatic Literary Work

HOW TO APPLY FOR COPYRIGHT REGISTRATION:

- *First:* Read the information on this page to make sure Form TX is the correct application for your work.

- *Second:* Open out the form by pulling this page to the left. Read through the detailed instructions before starting to complete the form.

- *Third:* Complete spaces 1-4 of the application, then turn the entire form over and, after reading the instructions for spaces 5-11, complete the rest of your application. Use typewriter or print in dark ink. Be sure to sign the form at space 10.

- *Fourth:* Detach your completed application from these instructions and send it with the necessary deposit of the work (see below) to: Register of Copyrights, Library of Congress, Washington, D.C. 20559. Unless you have a Deposit Account in the Copyright Office, your application and deposit must be accompanied by a check or money order for $10, payable to: *Register of Copyrights.*

WHEN TO USE FORM TX: Form TX is the appropriate application to use for copyright registration covering nondramatic literary works, whether published or unpublished.

WHAT IS A "NONDRAMATIC LITERARY WORK"? The category of "nondramatic literary works" (Class TX) is very broad. Except for dramatic works and certain kinds of audiovisual works. Class TX includes all types of works written in words (or other verbal or numerical symbols). A few of the many examples of "nondramatic literary works" include fiction, nonfiction, poetry, periodicals, textbooks, reference works, directories, catalogs, advertising copy, and compilations of information.

DEPOSIT TO ACCOMPANY APPLICATION: An application for copyright registration must be accompanied by a deposit representing the entire work for which registration is to be made. The following are the general deposit requirements as set forth in the statute:

Unpublished work: Deposit one complete copy (or phonorecord).

Published work: Deposit two complete copies (or phonorecords) of the best edition.

Work first published outside the United States: Deposit one complete copy (or phonorecord) of the first foreign edition.

Contribution to a collective work: Deposit one complete copy (or phonorecord) of the best edition of the collective work.

These general deposit requirements may vary in particular situations. For further information about copyright deposit, write to the Copyright Office.

THE COPYRIGHT NOTICE: For published works, the law provides that a copyright notice in a specified form "shall be placed on all publicly distributed copies from which the work can be visually perceived." Use of the copyright notice is the responsibility of the copyright owner and does not require advance permission from the Copyright Office. The required form of the notice for copies generally consists of three elements: (1) the symbol "©", or the word "Copyright", or the abbreviation "Copr."; (2) the year of first publication; and (3) the name of the owner of copyright. For example: "© 1978 Constance Porter" The notice is to be affixed to the copies "in such manner and location as to give reasonable notice of the claim of copyright." Unlike the law in effect before 1978, the new copyright statute provides procedures for correcting errors in the copyright notice, and even for curing the omission of the notice. However, a failure to comply with the notice requirements may still result in the loss of some copyright protection and, unless corrected within five years, in the complete loss of copyright. For further information about the copyright notice and the procedures for correcting errors or omissions, write to the Copyright Office.

DURATION OF COPYRIGHT: For works that were created after the effective date of the new statute (January 1, 1978), the basic copyright term will be the life of the author and fifty years after the author's death. For works made for hire, and for certain anonymous and pseudonymous works, the duration of copyright will be 75 years from publication or 100 years from creation, whichever is shorter. These same terms of copyright will generally apply to works that had been created before 1978 but had not been published or copyrighted before that date. For further information about the duration of copyright, including the terms of copyrights already in existence before 1978, write for Circular R15a.

FORM TX

UNITED STATES COPYRIGHT OFFICE

REGISTRATION NUMBER

TX   TXU

EFFECTIVE DATE OF REGISTRATION

....
Month   Day   Year

DO NOT WRITE ABOVE THIS LINE. IF YOU NEED MORE SPACE, USE CONTINUATION SHEET (FORM TX/CON)

①
Title

TITLE OF THIS WORK:

PREVIOUS OR ALTERNATIVE TITLES:

If a periodical or serial give Vol   No   Issue Date

PUBLICATION AS A CONTRIBUTION: (If this work was published as a contribution to a periodical, serial, or collection, give information about the collective work in which the contribution appeared.)

Title of Collective Work   Vol   No   Date .... Pages ......

②
Author(s)

IMPORTANT: Under the law, the "author" of a "work made for hire" is generally the employer, not the employee (see instructions). If any part of this work was "made for hire" check "Yes" in the space provided, give the employer (or other person for whom the work was prepared) as "Author" of that part, and leave the space for dates blank.

1

NAME OF AUTHOR:

DATES OF BIRTH AND DEATH:
Born .... Died ....
(Year)   (Year)

Was this author's contribution to the work a "work made for hire"?   Yes   No

AUTHOR'S NATIONALITY OR DOMICILE:
Citizen of .... or { Domiciled in ....
(Name of Country)   (Name of Country)

WAS THIS AUTHOR'S CONTRIBUTION TO THE WORK:
Anonymous?   Yes   No
Pseudonymous?   Yes   No
If the answer to either of these questions is "Yes," see detailed instructions attached

AUTHOR OF: (Briefly describe nature of this author's contribution)

2

NAME OF AUTHOR:

DATES OF BIRTH AND DEATH:
Born .... Died ....
(Year)   (Year)

Was this author's contribution to the work a "work made for hire"?   Yes   No

AUTHOR'S NATIONALITY OR DOMICILE:
Citizen of .... or { Domiciled in ....
(Name of Country)   (Name of Country)

WAS THIS AUTHOR'S CONTRIBUTION TO THE WORK:
Anonymous?   Yes   No
Pseudonymous?   Yes   No
If the answer to either of these questions is "Yes," see detailed instructions attached

AUTHOR OF: (Briefly describe nature of this author's contribution)

3

NAME OF AUTHOR:

DATES OF BIRTH AND DEATH:
Born .... Died ....
(Year)   (Year)

Was this author's contribution to the work a "work made for hire"?   Yes   No

AUTHOR'S NATIONALITY OR DOMICILE:
Citizen of .... or { Domiciled in ....
(Name of Country)   (Name of Country)

WAS THIS AUTHOR'S CONTRIBUTION TO THE WORK:
Anonymous?   Yes   No
Pseudonymous?   Yes   No
If the answer to either of these questions is "Yes," see detailed instructions attached

AUTHOR OF: (Briefly describe nature of this author's contribution)

③
Creation and Publication

YEAR IN WHICH CREATION OF THIS WORK WAS COMPLETED:

Year
(This information must be given in all cases.)

DATE AND NATION OF FIRST PUBLICATION:

Date ....
(Month)   (Day)   (Year)

Nation ....
(Name of Country)
(Complete this block ONLY if this work has been published.)

④
Claimant(s)

NAME(S) AND ADDRESS(ES) OF COPYRIGHT CLAIMANT(S):

TRANSFER: (If the copyright claimant(s) named here in space 4 are different from the author(s) named in space 2, give a brief statement of how the claimant(s) obtained ownership of the copyright.)

• Complete all applicable spaces (numbers 5-11) on the reverse side of this page
• Follow detailed instructions attached   • Sign the form at line 10

DO NOT WRITE HERE

Page 1 of .... pages

115

HOW TO FILL OUT FORM TX

Specific Instructions for Spaces 1-4

- The line-by-line instructions on this page are keyed to the spaces on the first page of Form TX, printed opposite.
- Please read through these instructions before you start filling out your application, and refer to the specific instructions for each space as you go along.

SPACE 1: TITLE

- **Title of this Work:** Every work submitted for copyright registration must be given a title that is capable of identifying that particular work. If the copies or phonorecords of the work bear a title (or an identifying phrase that could serve as a title), transcribe its wording completely and exactly on the application. Remember that indexing of the registration and future identification of the work will depend on the information you give here.

- **Periodical or Serial Issue:** Periodicals and other serials are publications issued at intervals under a general title, such as newspapers, magazines, journals, newsletters, and annuals. If the work being registered is an entire issue of a periodical or serial, give the over-all title of the periodical or serial in the space headed "Title of this Work," and add the specific information about the issue in

the spaces provided. If the work being registered is a contribution to a periodical or serial issue, follow the instructions for "Publication as a Contribution."

- **Previous or Alternative Titles:** Complete this space if there are any additional titles for the work under which someone searching for the registration might be likely to look, or under which a document pertaining to the work might be recorded.

- **Publication as a Contribution:** If the work being registered has been published as a contribution to a periodical, serial, or collection, give the title of the contribution in the space headed "Title of this Work." Then, in the line headed "Publication as a Contribution," give information about the larger work in which the contribution appeared.

SPACE 2: AUTHORS

- **General Instructions:** First decide, after reading these instructions, who are the "authors" of this work for copyright purposes. Then, unless the work is a "collective work" (see below), give the requested information about every "author" who contributed any appreciable amount of copyrightable matter to this version of the work. If you need further space, use the attached Continuation Sheet and, if necessary, request additional Continuation Sheets (Form TX/CON).

- **Who is the "Author"?** Unless the work was "made for hire," the individual who actually created the work is its "author." In the case of a work made for hire, the statute provides that "the employer or other person for whom the work was prepared is considered the author."

- **What is a "Work Made for Hire"?** A "work made for hire" is defined as: (1) "a work prepared by an employee within the scope of his or her employment", or (2) "a work specially ordered or commissioned" for certain uses specified in the statute, but only if there is a written agreement to consider it a "work made for hire."

- **Collective Work:** In the case of a collective work, such as a periodical issue, anthology, collection of essays, or encyclopedia, it is sufficient to give information about the author of the collective work as a whole.

- **Author's Identity Not Revealed:** If an author's contribution is "anonymous" or "pseudonymous," it is not necessary to give the name and dates for that author. However, the citizenship or domicile of the author **must** be given in all cases, and information about the nature of that author's contribution to the work should be included.

- **Name of Author:** The fullest form of the author's name should be given. If

you have checked "Yes" to indicate that the work was "made for hire," give the full legal name of the employer (or other person for whom the work was prepared). You may also include the name of the employee (for example, "Elster Publishing Co., employer for hire of John Ferguson"). If the work is "anonymous" you may: (1) leave the line blank, or (2) state "Anonymous" in the line, or (3) reveal the author's identity. If the work is "pseudonymous" you may (1) leave the line blank, or (2) give the pseudonym and identify it as such (for example: "Huntley Haverstock, pseudonym"), or (3) reveal the author's name, making clear which is the real name and which is the pseudonym (for example, "Judith Barton, whose pseudonym is Madeleine Elster").

- **Dates of Birth and Death:** If the author is dead, the statute requires that the year of death be included in the application unless the work is anonymous or pseudonymous. The author's birth date is optional, but is useful as a form of identification. Leave this space blank if the author's contribution was a "work made for hire."

- **"Anonymous" or "Pseudonymous" Work:** An author's contribution to a work is "anonymous" if that author is not identified on the copies or phonorecords of the work. An author's contribution to a work is "pseudonymous" if that author is identified on the copies or phonorecords under a fictitious name.

- **Author's Nationality or Domicile:** Give the country of which the author is a citizen, or the country in which the author is domiciled. The statute requires that either nationality or domicile be given in all cases.

- **Nature of Authorship:** After the words "Author of" give a brief general statement of the nature of this particular author's contribution to the work. Examples: "Entire text", "Co-author of entire text", "Chapters 11-14", "Editorial revisions", "Compilation and English translation", "Illustrations".

SPACE 3: CREATION AND PUBLICATION

- **General Instructions:** Do not confuse "creation" with "publication." Every application for copyright registration must state "the year in which creation of the work was completed." Give the date and nation of first publication only if the work has been published.

- **Creation:** Under the statute, a work is "created" when it is fixed in a copy or phonorecord for the first time. Where a work has been prepared over a period of time, the part of the work existing in fixed form on a particular date constitutes the created work on that date. The date you give here should be the year in which the author completed the particular version for which registration

is now being sought, even if other versions exist or if further changes or additions are planned.

- **Publication:** The statute defines "publication" as "the distribution of copies or phonorecords of a work to the public by sale or other transfer of ownership, or by rental, lease, or lending"; a work is also "published" if there has been an "offering to distribute copies or phonorecords to a group of persons for purposes of further distribution, public performance, or public display." Give the full date (month, day, year) when, and the country where, publication first occurred. If first publication took place simultaneously in the United States and other countries, it is sufficient to state "U.S.A."

SPACE 4: CLAIMANT(S)

- **Name(s) and Address(es) of Copyright Claimant(s):** Give the name(s) address(es) of the copyright claimant(s) in this work. The statute provides that copyright in a work belongs initially to the author of the work (including, in the case of a work made for hire, the employer or other person for whom the work was prepared). The copyright claimant is either the author of the work or a person or organization that has obtained ownership of the copyright initially belonging to the author.

- **Transfer:** The statute provides that, if the copyright claimant is not the author, the application for registration must contain "a brief statement of how the claimant obtained ownership of the copyright." If any copyright claimant named in space 4 is not an author named in space 2, give a brief, general statement summarizing the means by which that claimant obtained ownership of the copyright.

116

EXAMINED BY:	APPLICATION RECEIVED:	
CHECKED BY:		FOR COPYRIGHT OFFICE USE ONLY
CORRESPONDENCE ☐ Yes	DEPOSIT RECEIVED:	
DEPOSIT ACCOUNT FUNDS USED: ☐	REMITTANCE NUMBER AND DATE:	

DO NOT WRITE ABOVE THIS LINE. IF YOU NEED ADDITIONAL SPACE, USE CONTINUATION SHEET (FORM TX/CON)

PREVIOUS REGISTRATION:

- Has registration for this work, or for an earlier version of this work, already been made in the Copyright Office?   **Yes**   **No**
- If your answer is "Yes," why is another registration being sought? (Check appropriate box)
  - ☐ This is the first published edition of a work previously registered in unpublished form
  - ☐ This is the first application submitted by this author as copyright claimant
  - ☐ This is a changed version of the work, as shown by line 6 of this application
- If your answer is "Yes," give: Previous Registration Number _____ Year of Registration _____

⑤ Previous Registration

COMPILATION OR DERIVATIVE WORK: (See instructions)

PREEXISTING MATERIAL. (Identify any preexisting work or works that this work is based on or incorporates.)

{

MATERIAL ADDED TO THIS WORK. (Give a brief, general statement of the material that has been added to this work and in which copyright is claimed.)

{

⑥ Compilation or Derivative Work

MANUFACTURERS AND LOCATIONS: (If this is a published work consisting preponderantly of nondramatic literary material in English, the law may require that the copies be manufactured in the United States or Canada for full protection. If so, the names of the manufacturers who performed certain processes, and the places where these processes were performed must be given. See instructions for details.)

NAMES OF MANUFACTURERS   PLACES OF MANUFACTURE

⑦ Manufacturing

REPRODUCTION FOR USE OF BLIND OR PHYSICALLY-HANDICAPPED PERSONS: (See instructions)

- Signature of this form at space 10, and a check in one of the boxes here in space 8, constitutes a non exclusive grant of permission to the Library of Congress to reproduce and distribute solely for the blind and physically handicapped and under the conditions and limitations prescribed by the regulations of the Copyright Office (1) copies of the work identified in space 1 of this application in Braille (or similar tactile symbols), or (2) phonorecords embodying a fixation of a reading of that work, or (3) both

  a ☐ Copies and phonorecords   b ☐ Copies Only   c ☐ Phonorecords Only

⑧ License For Handicapped

DEPOSIT ACCOUNT: (If the registration fee is to be charged to a Deposit Account established in the Copyright Office, give name and number of Account.)

Name: _____
Account Number: _____

CORRESPONDENCE: (Give name and address to which correspondence about this application should be sent.)

Name _____
Address: _____ (Apt.)
(City) (State) (ZIP)

⑨ Fee and Correspondence

CERTIFICATION: ✳ I, the undersigned, hereby certify that I am the: (Check one)

☐ author ☐ other copyright claimant ☐ owner of exclusive right(s) ☐ authorized agent of _____
(Name of author or other copyright claimant, or owner of exclusive right(s))

of the work identified in this application and that the statements made by me in this application are correct to the best of my knowledge.

☞ Handwritten signature: (X) _____

Typed or printed name _____ Date _____

⑩ Certification (Application must be signed)

... (Name) ...	**MAIL CERTIFICATE TO**	**⑪ Address For Return of Certificate**
... (Number, Street and Apartment Number) ...		
... (City) (State) (ZIP code) ...	(Certificate will be mailed in window envelope)	

✳ 17 U S C § 506(e) Any person who knowingly makes a false representation of a material fact in the application for copyright registration provided for by section 409, or in any written statement filed in connection with the application, shall be fined not more than $2,500

◉ U.S. GOVERNMENT PRINTING OFFICE: 1980: 311-425/3

Jan. 1980—500,000

INSTRUCTIONS FOR FILLING OUT SPACES 5-11 OF FORM TX

SPACE 5: PREVIOUS REGISTRATION

• **General Instructions:** The questions in space 5 are intended to find out whether an earlier registration has been made for this work and, if so, whether there is any basis for a new registration. As a general rule, only one basic copyright registration can be made for the same version of a particular work.

• **Same Version:** If this version is substantially the same as the work covered by a previous registration, a second registration is not generally possible unless: (1) the work has been registered in unpublished form and a second registration is now being sought to cover the first published edition, or (2) someone other than the author is identified as copyright claimant in the earlier registration, and the author is now seeking registration in his or her own name. If either

of these two exceptions apply, check the appropriate box and give the earlier registration number and date. Otherwise, do not submit Form TX; instead, write the Copyright Office for information about supplementary registration or recordation of transfers of copyright ownership.

• **Changed Version:** If the work has been changed, and you are now seeking registration to cover the additions or revisions, check the third box in space 5, give the earlier registration number and date, and complete both parts of space 6.

• **Previous Registration Number and Date:** If more than one previous registration has been made for the work, give the number and date of the latest registration.

SPACE 6: COMPILATION OR DERIVATIVE WORK

• **General Instructions:** Complete both parts of space 6 if this work is a "compilation," or "derivative work," or both, and if it incorporates one or more earlier works that have already been published or registered for copyright, or that have fallen into the public domain. A "compilation" is defined as "a work formed by the collection and assembling of preexisting materials or of data that are selected, coordinated, or arranged in such a way that the resulting work as a whole constitutes an original work of authorship." A "derivative work" is "a work based on one or more preexisting works." Examples of derivative works include translations, fictionalizations, arrangements, abridgments, condensations, or "any other form in which a work may be recast, transformed, or adapted." Derivative works also include works "consisting of editorial revisions, annotations, elaborations, or other modifications" if these changes, as a whole, represent an original work of authorship.

• **Preexisting Material:** If the work is a compilation, give a brief, general statement describing the nature of the material that has been compiled. Example: "Compilation of all published 1917 speeches of Woodrow Wilson." In the case of a derivative work, identify the preexisting work that has been recast, transformed, or adapted. Example: "Russian version of Goncharov's 'Oblomov'."

• **Material Added to this Work:** The statute requires a "brief, general statement of the additional material covered by the copyright claim being registered." This statement should describe all of the material in this particular version of the work that: (1) represents an original work of authorship; and (2) has not fallen into the public domain; and (3) has not been previously published; and (4) has not been previously registered for copyright in unpublished form. Examples: "Foreword, selection, arrangement, editing, critical annotations"; "Revisions throughout; chapters 11-17 entirely new".

SPACE 7: MANUFACTURING PROVISIONS

• **General Instructions:** The copyright statute currently provides, as a general rule, and with a number of exceptions, that the copies of a published work "consisting preponderantly of nondramatic literary material that is in the English language" be manufactured in the United States in order to be lawfully imported and publicly distributed in the United States. At the present time, applications for copyright registration covering published works that consist mainly of nondramatic text matter in English must, in most cases, identify those who performed certain processes in manufacturing the copies, together with the places where those processes were performed. Please note: The information must be given even if the copies were manufactured outside the United States or Canada; registration will be made regardless of the places of manufacture identified in space 7. In general, the processes covered

by this provision are: (1) typesetting and plate-making (where a typographic process preceded the actual printing); (2) the making of plates by a lithographic or photoengraving process (where this was a final or intermediate step before printing); and (3) the final printing and binding processes (in all cases). Leave space 7 blank if your work is unpublished or is not in English.

• **Import Statement:** As an exception to the manufacturing provisions, the statute prescribes that, where manufacture has taken place outside the United States or Canada, a maximum of 2000 copies of the foreign edition can be imported into the United States without affecting the copyright owner's rights. For this purpose, the Copyright Office will issue an import statement upon request and payment of a fee of $3 at the time of registration or at any later time. For further information about import statements, ask for Form IS.

SPACE 8: REPRODUCTION FOR USE OF BLIND OR PHYSICALLY-HANDICAPPED PERSONS

• **General Instructions:** One of the major programs of the Library of Congress is to provide Braille editions and special recordings of works for the exclusive use of the blind and physically handicapped. In an effort to simplify and speed up the copyright licensing procedures that are a necessary part of this program, section 710 of the copyright statute provides for the establishment of a voluntary licensing system to be tied in with copyright registration. Under this system, the owner of copyright in a nondramatic literary work has the option, at the time of registration on Form TX, to grant to the Library of Congress a license to reproduce and distribute Braille editions and "talking books" or "talking magazines" of the work being registered. The Copyright Office regulations

provide that, under the license, the reproduction and distribution must be solely for the use of persons who are certified by competent authority as unable to read normal printed material as a result of physical limitations. The license is nonexclusive, and may be terminated upon 90 days notice. For further information, write for Circular R63.

• **How to Grant the License:** The license is entirely voluntary. If you wish to grant it, check one of the three boxes in space 8. Your check in one of these boxes, together with your signature in space 10, will mean that the Library of Congress can proceed to reproduce and distribute under the license without further paperwork.

SPACES 9, 10, 11: FEE, CORRESPONDENCE, CERTIFICATION, RETURN ADDRESS

• **Deposit Account and Mailing Instructions (Space 9):** If you maintain a Deposit Account in the Copyright Office, identify it in space 9. Otherwise you will need to send the registration fee of $10 with your application. The space headed "Correspondence" should contain the name and address of the person to be consulted if correspondence about this application becomes necessary.

• **Certification (Space 10):** The application is not acceptable unless it bears the handwritten signature of the author or other copyright claimant, or of the owner of exclusive right(s), or of the duly authorized agent of such author, claimant, or owner.

• **Address for Return of Certificate (Space 11):** The address box must be completed legibly, since the certificate will be returned in a window envelope.

ADJUNCT APPLICATION
for
Copyright Registration for a Group of Contributions to Periodicals

- Use this adjunct form only if your are making a single registration for a group of contributions to periodicals, and you are also filing a basic application on Form TX, Form PA, or Form VA. Follow the instructions, attached.
- Number each line in Part B consecutively. Use additional Forms GR/CP if you need more space.
- Submit this adjunct form with the basic application form. Clip (do not tape or staple) and fold all sheets together before submitting them.

FORM GR/CP
UNITED STATES COPYRIGHT OFFICE

REGISTRATION NUMBER		
TX	PA	VA

EFFECTIVE DATE OF REGISTRATION

(Month)	(Day)	(Year)

FORM GR/CP RECEIVED

Page _____ of _____ pages

DO NOT WRITE ABOVE THIS LINE. FOR COPYRIGHT OFFICE USE ONLY

(A)
Identification of Application

IDENTIFICATION OF BASIC APPLICATION:
- This application for copyright registration for a group of contributions to periodicals is submitted as an adjunct to an application filed on: (Check which)

☐ Form TX   ☐ Form PA   ☐ Form VA

IDENTIFICATION OF AUTHOR AND CLAIMANT: (Give the name of the author and the name of the copyright claimant in all of the contributions listed in Part B of this form. The names should be the same as the names given in spaces 2 and 4 of the basic application.)

Name of Author:

Name of Copyright Claimant:

(B)
Registration For Group of Contributions

COPYRIGHT REGISTRATION FOR A GROUP OF CONTRIBUTIONS TO PERIODICALS: (To make a single registration for a group of works by the same individual author, all first published as contributions to periodicals within a 12 month period (see instructions), give full information about each contribution. If more space is needed, use additional Forms GR/CP.)

☐ Title of Contribution:
Title of Periodical: Vol.   No.   Issue Date   Pages
Date of First Publication: (Month)   (Day)   (Year)   Nation of First Publication   (Country)

☐ Title of Contribution:
Title of Periodical: Vol.   No.   Issue Date   Pages
Date of First Publication: (Month)   (Day)   (Year)   Nation of First Publication   (Country)

☐ Title of Contribution:
Title of Periodical: Vol.   No.   Issue Date   Pages
Date of First Publication: (Month)   (Day)   (Year)   Nation of First Publication   (Country)

☐ Title of Contribution:
Title of Periodical: Vol.   No.   Issue Date   Pages
Date of First Publication: (Month)   (Day)   (Year)   Nation of First Publication   (Country)

☐ Title of Contribution:
Title of Periodical: Vol.   No.   Issue Date   Pages
Date of First Publication: (Month)   (Day)   (Year)   Nation of First Publication   (Country)

☐ Title of Contribution:
Title of Periodical: Vol.   No.   Issue Date   Pages
Date of First Publication: (Month)   (Day)   (Year)   Nation of First Publication   (Country)

☐ Title of Contribution:
Title of Periodical: Vol.   No.   Issue Date   Pages
Date of First Publication: (Month)   (Day)   (Year)   Nation of First Publication   (Country)

119

FORM GR/CP

UNITED STATES COPYRIGHT OFFICE
LIBRARY OF CONGRESS
WASHINGTON, D.C. 20559

THIS FORM:

- Can be used solely as an adjunct to a basic application for copyright registration.
- Is not acceptable unless submitted together with Form TX, Form PA, or Form VA.
- Is acceptable only if the group of works listed on it all qualify for a single copyright registration under 17 U.S.C. § 408 (c)(2).

ADJUNCT APPLICATION
for Copyright Registration for a
Group of Contributions to Periodicals

WHEN TO USE FORM GR/CP: Form GR/CP is the appropriate adjunct application form to use when you are submitting a basic application on Form TX, Form PA, or Form VA, for a group of works that qualify for a single registration under section 408(c)(2) of the copyright statute.

WHEN DOES A GROUP OF WORKS QUALIFY FOR A SINGLE REGISTRATION OR UNDER 17 U.S.C. §408 (c)(2)? The statute provides that a single copyright registration for a group of works can be made if **all** of the following conditions are met:

(1) All of the works are by the same author, who is an individual (not an employer for hire); and

(2) All of the works were first published as contributions to periodicals (including newspapers) within a twelve-month period; and

(3) Each of the contributions as first published bore a separate copyright notice, and the name of the owner of copyright in the work (or an abbreviation or alternative designation of the owner) was the same in each notice; and

(4) One copy of the entire periodical issue or newspaper section in which each contribution was first published must be deposited with the application; and

(5) The application must identify each contribution separately, including the periodical containing it and the date of its first publication.

How to Apply for Group Registration:

First: Study the information on this page to make sure that all of the works you want to register together as a group qualify for a single registration.

Second: Turn this page over and read through the detailed instructions for group registration. Decide which form you should use for the basic registration (Form TX for nondramatic literary works; or Form PA for musical, dramatic, and other works of the performing arts; or Form VA for pictorial and graphic works). Be sure that you have all of the information you need before you start filling out both the basic and the adjunct application forms.

Third: Complete the basic application form, following the detailed instructions accompanying it **and the special instructions on the reverse of this page**.

Fourth: Complete the adjunct application on Form GR/CP and mail it, together with the basic application form and the required copy of each contribution, to: Register of Copyrights, Library of Congress, Washington, D.C. 20559. Unless you have a Deposit Account in the Copyright Office, your application and copies must be accompanied by a check or money order for $10, payable to: *Register of Copyrights.*

120

The articles listed must all have been published within a twelve-month period, although the twelve months do not have to be a calendar year. You must send a copy of each periodical or newspaper section in which the article was first published. The fee is ten dollars no matter how many contributions you list, as long as they appeared within a twelve-month period.

According to the 1976 Act, you must also place a copyright notice "on all publicly distributed copies from which the work can be perceived." This is the government's way of saying that any copyrighted material must contain:

1. The symbol © or the word *Copyright*, or the abbreviation "copr."

2. The first year of publication or, for unpublished works, the year the article was created.

3. The name of the owner of the copyright, for example, © 1980 Charlotte Beauregard. The Act does not specify where to put the copyright notice, but the notice must be clearly visible on the document. Bottom left- or right-hand corner is best.

FAIR USE— YOUR RIGHT TO SOMEONE ELSE'S MATERIAL

"How much material can I use from another source before I must ask permission?" is a common fair use question. Protecting yourself against the charge that you have unfairly used someone's material is easy—just write for permission whenever you have a trickle of a doubt that what you want to use exceeds the boundaries of fair use.

According to the 1976 Copyright Act, four factors should be included in any judgment of whether the use made of any work is "fair." These factors are:

1. The purpose and character of the use, including whether such use is of a commercial nature or is for nonprofit educational purposes.

2. The nature of the copyrighted work.

3. The amount and substantiality of the portion used in relation to the copyrighted work as a whole.

4. The effect of the use upon the potential market for, or value of, the copyrighted work.

Chances that you could be charged with an infringement of fair use improve, then, if what you want to use is commercially marketed, if the copyrighted work is clearly covered by the Copyright Act, or if you use a large portion of the work, which may interfere with the author's ability to market the work in the future.

Printing an entire chapter from a book or using a Mickey Mouse logo without permission are obvious copyright infringements. Less clear is the use of several paragraphs from a source you need for an article.

Credit should always be given to quoted material, either in a footnote (although rarely is this magazine style) or in an acknowledgment preceding or following the quote (such as "According to Timothy Crouse in *The Boys on the Bus*, . . ."). The facts in a news or feature story (who, what, why, where, when, and how) are not copyrightable, but the arrangement of those facts is. A standard practice among writers quoting material from a magazine or newspaper article is the 250-word rule. Two hundred and fifty words used with acknowledgment of the source usually does not require permission. If, however, 250 words is a substantial core of the article, write for permission.

No absolute rules exist about the amount of material you may use. Here are some guidlines, *used with permission*, from the revised *Prentice-Hall Author's Guide*, fifth edition (Englewood Cliffs, N. J.: Prentice-Hall, 1978):

> *If you are quoting from a* textbook, *our guidelines permit use of up to 250 words without permission (except for charts and tables and material to be used in anthologies). In all cases, be sure to credit the source. All quotations of more than 250 words—and that means total number of words from one source, possibly in scattered quotes—require written permission.*

The quotation does not have to be exact to require permission; even if the material is paraphrased or adapted, get permission to use it in that form.

Our guidelines require written permission for quotations of fewer than 250 words under the following circumstances:

1. If the quotation is from a trade book (a book for the general public), obtain permission to use any quotation, whatever its length.

2. If the quotation exceeds 5 percent of the entire work from which it is taken—for example, if 135 words are taken from an essay of 2500 words.

3. If the quotation is poetry. No more than two lines should be used without permission, unless two lines constitute a stanza; then we require permission to quote even that amount.

4. If the quotation is to be used in an anthology or compilation, permission should be obtained for *every selection* in copyright, no matter how short.

5. If the quotation is from an unpublished work—for example, a thesis, lecture, or material prepared by a student as part of a course.

6. If the quotation is from a letter, published or unpublished. If the letter has been published under a copyright that has now expired, no permission is necessary. But if it is protected by a copyright still in force, written permission to quote from it is needed. For example, it is not safe to use a letter by Abraham Lincoln without investigation—it may have been published many years after it was written and may still be in copyright. If a letter has never been published, get the permission of the *writer* (not of the person to whom it was written) to quote from it. If the writer is dead, get the permission of whoever owns the right to publish the writer's literary legacy. If you solicit letters for publication, put your request in writing, making it clear that they are to be published.

7. If the quotation consists of music, either popular or classical, or of song lyrics that are still in copyright. Be careful of arrangements of old classical or folk music and lyrics. They are usually copyrighted.

8. If the quotation is a chart or table—or an adaption thereof.

9. If the quotation is from a copyrighted dramatic composition, such as a play, motion picture film, or TV presentation.

10. If the quotation is used in an ornamental way (for example, as part of a chapter opening design).

Fiction, speeches, columns, editorials, syndicated material, illustrations, and photographs are also covered by the new copyright law. So, be safe and ask permission from a newspaper if you plan to use a lengthy excerpt or from the artist or photographer if you plan to reprint an illustration or a photograph.

Ideas cannot be copyrighted, nor can titles or United States government documents. If the United States government uses copyrighted material in one of its documents, however, you should write to the original holder of copyright for that material if you want to use the larger government document. This means that you can reproduce a government booklet on health, for instance, but if the booklet reprints an article from the *New York Times,* you must write to the *Times* for permission to reproduce the *Times* article in what you write.

To request approval, send a letter of permission to the person or the organization that originated the article (see Sample Permission Request). A letter to an organization should be addressed in care of the Permissions Department. Type the letter in triplicate and keep a copy, sending two copies to the copyright holder. This allows the holder to keep a record of the approved passage, pages, or illustration. Include an SASE.

Permissions can take a week to a month, even longer. Most requests are routinely approved, but some copyright holders will request a fee, which leaves you to decide whether you want to pay the fee or drop the item from your article. Because this process can

---

*It should be understood that these are merely our [Prentice Hall's] *guidelines.* They should not be considered determinative of what does or does not constitute "fair use" in the legal sense, in every case.

take time, write for permission as soon as you realize you want to use something covered by copyright. Otherwise, the lack of a signed permission request will keep you from mailing your article on time.

Sample Permission Request

Your Address
City, State, Zip
Date

Name
Address
City, State, Zip

Dear _____:

I am preparing an article entitled _____ _____ for _____. May I have your permission to include the following:

(text of what is to be included)

in my article and in future revisions thereof, including nonexclusive world rights in all languages. This permission in no way restricts republication of your material in any form by you or by others authorized by you.

Unless you indicate otherwise, I will use the following credit line:

© *date* by _____. Reprinted by permission.

Please sign and return this permission form to me by __(date)__ so that I can meet my deadline.

I have included one copy for your records.

Thank you,

Your Name

LIBEL AND SLANDER

The concepts of libel and slander in the United States derive from the English common law idea of defamation. Interpreted by American courts, this means that the First Amendment to the Constitution protecting freedom of speech is not "a license to circulate damaging falsehoods or personal attacks on a person in the guise of news gathering and informing the public," according to Ella Cooper Thomas.[1]

Libel is defamation in print; slander concerns only oral comments. To be libelous, defamatory remarks must be a "communication which exposes a person to hatred, ridicule, or contempt, lowers him in the esteem of his fellows, causes him to be shunned, or injures him in his business or calling."[2] The libelous remarks also must be communicated to a third party, and publication of such remarks obviously meets this requirement.

The laws governing libel are a very complex tug-of-war, described by legal scholar William L. Prosser as "the conflict of opposing ideas of policy in which traditional notions of freedom of expression have collided violently with sympathy for the victim traduced and indignation at the maligning tongue."[3] State court interpretations have added more confusion to this legal stew, so that what may be considered libelous differs from state to state.

Although most daily newspapers and other publications may be able to consult an attorney before publishing an article with any tint of controversy, as a magazine writer you probably cannot. Yet, as a writer you are responsible, and you can be named in a libel action, along with the editor, the owner, and in some states even the printer who publishes the article.[4]

There are four defenses against the charge of libel.

[1]Ella Cooper Thomas, *The Law of Libel and Slander* (Dobbs Ferry, N. Y.: Oceana Publications, 1973), p. 5.

[2]Harold Nelson and Dwight Teeter, *Law of Mass Communication* (Mineola, N. Y.: Foundation Press, 1969), p. 44.

[3]William L. Prosser, *Law of Torts*, 4th ed. (St. Paul, Minn.: West Publishing, 1971), p. 737.

[4]Thomas, *Law of Libel and Slander*, pp. 23–24.

1. *Truth*—that the published remarks can be proven to be true.

2. *Qualified privilege*—that the social good of the community served by publishing the information overrides the damage done to an individual reputation.

3. *Absolute privilege*—that the comments were made by individuals testifying at judicial and legislative hearings.

4. *Fair comment and criticism*—that the writer was commenting or criticizing matters of public concern.[5]

The defense of fair comment was broadened by the 1964 *New York Times* v. *Sullivan* case, which found that a public official cannot collect damages for defamation about his or her official duties unless the charges were made with "actual malice—that is with knowledge that it was false or with reckless disregard of whether it was false or not."[6]

This decision was key in the concept of defining malice, and subsequent decisions also expanded the definition of public officials to include public figures. Thus, the law differentiates between public and private persons as subjects of fair comment and criticism. This fluid defense continues to be defined, and may even be limited, by future decisions.

There are ways that you, as a magazine writer, can protect yourself against liability.

1. Always check the facts thoroughly. Compared to a newspaper reporter, you have more time to be accurate. On particularly sensitive issues, two sources of information may not be enough to verify a fact. Find more.

2. Personal criticism of an individual's character or abilities should, whenever possible, be attributed with direct quotes rather than be credited to "some critics" or "someone who should know."

[5]Prosser, *Law of Torts*, pp. 776–792.
[6]*New York Times* v. *Sullivan*, 376 U. S. 245 (1964).

3. Whenever you write literary criticism, aim your comments strictly at the book or play as art.

4. When you write commentary, limit yourself to the issues. Personal attacks are unnecessary in a thoughtful critical argument, and they make you legally vulnerable.

5. Whenever you are nervous about the possible liability of an article you have written, tell the magazine for which you are writing, but also find good legal counsel to review the article *before* you submit it. Do not count on the magazine editors to protect your interests.

In practice, few magazine writers ever face liability for what they write. Your articles will concentrate on feature material, where your interviewees consent, even rush, to help you. But do not jeopardize your craft with quick judgments in a questionable situation. Caution is crucial.

RIGHT TO PRIVACY

Newsworthiness of the subject has often been used as a defense against the right to privacy, as well as a defense against libel. A person's right to privacy sometimes conflicts with the public's right to know.

Publishing a photograph or a likeness that implies a person's commercial endorsement of a product is an invasion of privacy. Knowingly publishing nondefamatory but false information can violate someone's right to privacy. So can the publication of private or embarrassing facts.

This is a legal tightrope, and if you find yourself walking it, check with an attorney.

FOR MORE INFORMATION

To learn more about copyright, read *The Nuts and Bolts of Copyright*, available free from the Copyright Office, Library of Congress, Washington, D. C. 20559.

For a good overview of all the legal issues facing the writer, read *Law and the Writer*, edited by Kirk Polking and Leonard S. Meranus (Writer's Digest 1978, second edition), *A Copyright Guide* by Don Johnston (R. R. Bowker 1977), and *New Strategies for Public Affairs Reporting* by George S. Hage, Everette E. Dennis, Arnold H. Ismack, and Stephen Hortgen (Prentice-Hall 1976).

The books listed in the footnotes throughout this chapter will also be helpful. But always remember—when in doubt, check with an attorney.

12

The Final Draft

Many states have legislated a three-day "cooling off" period for financial transactions, which allows you to reconsider your decision. Writers should allow themselves at least the same amount of time to overcome their enthusiasm for their own brilliance, creativity, and wit. Humility helps.

CHECKPOINTS

Now that you are willing to desecrate this monument that is your article, check the following:

1. Organization. Now is the time to retrieve those scissors and tape from the supply pile. Does one paragraph belong before another? Have you used a new term before explaining it? Rearrange your article on your floor or desk by cutting it into pieces and putting the pieces back the way you want them. You can make a copy and cut up the copy, which saves your original organization (in case you decide that the way you originally organized your article was best).

2. Verification. Have you checked the spelling for all names and verified all statistics? One writer was humiliated when his article on a former *Playboy* Bunny appeared and all she could remember was that he misspelled her name.

3. Theme. Does every sentence, every paragraph contribute to your theme?

4. Audience. Is your language appropriate for your readers? Are you too colloquial, too stilted, or too filled with jargon?

BIG PROBLEMS— GOBBLEDYGOOK, CLICHES, AND QUOTATIONS

Gobbledygook. Would you rather "start" than "proceed in an ongoing direction?" Would you rather "do your best" then "maximize your present opportunities to succeed?"

If so, you are an enemy of gobbledygook, a form of government jargon that allows people to say nothing at length. We are all inheritors of this abuse of language, so watch for its uncanny ability to creep into your writing.

Some examples are:

Gobbledygook: Slow all forward motion until progress is terminated.

Translation: Stop.

Gobbledygook: Time-payment differential.

Translation: Finance charge.

Gobbledygook: The occupational incidence of the demand change is unlikely to coincide with the occupational profile of those registered at the employment office.

Translation: The jobs may not fit the people.

Gobbledygook: The perceptive data were analyzed through use of a content analysis methodology.

Translation: I looked at it.

Some government officials have, of course, made attempts to clear up the confusion. Wrote one government executive:

> *It has been mentioned by the Director that a significant number of letters prepared for his signature are too wordy and redundant. He is also concerned that some of our letters in response to correspondence from the general public are somewhat caustic and authoritarian . . . . All letters going outside the Department should be direct and to the point and avoid language which would be irritating or harsh to the reader.*[1]

Translation: Keep your writing helpful and concise.

Cliches. In a world of mass media, upbeat and repeatable phrases can slip into our language in a short time. "What can you say?" or "You know" grow trite quickly. Equally trite are cliches, those phrases or expressions that have spent so much time in our language that they are now boring. A cliche is the first sign of a tired writer. And your reader will be just as bored reading a cliche as you should be writing one. Some examples are:

It's all *water under the bridge.*

Like finding a *needle in a haystack.*

It's just a *can of worms.*

She's the *apple of his eye.*

He will call *in the not too distant future* (which can also qualify as gobbledygook for *soon*).

William Overend can spot a cliche a mile away:

> Eric Elfman is just a shade over 18. He has a ready smile, a way with words, and he knows a good thing when he sees one.
>
> Recently he won the "Great American Cliche Contest," which entitles him to a week of fun in the sun for two at the fabulous Fontainebleau Hotel in Miami Beach.

[1]Shirley Biagi, "Obfuscation Needs Clarification," *The Barascope*, January-February 1974. Courtesy *The Barascope*, a publication of NL Baroid, NL Industries, Inc.

"I couldn't believe it when I heard the news," Elfman recalled this week in a rare, exclusive interview. "It was like a dream come true."

The tension had been mounting for months. Elfman had seen an ad for the contest at a bookstore in Westwood. It was a promotion for a book called "The Great American Cliche" by Lawrence Paros.

"I didn't want good fortune to pass me by," Elfman said. "I guess you could say I was ready when opportunity knocked."

Elfman didn't waste any time getting started. He hopped a bus back to his apartment in Westchester, just a stone's throw from the Los Angeles Airport.

As he bent over his typewriter, his mind teeming with cliches, he could see the giant silver birds lifting slowly off the tarmac. But Elfman barely noticed. He was buried in his work.

This is what he wrote, the fruit of his labors, a brief but poignant detective story that helped make Elfman what he is today:

"It was a dark and lonely night when she walked into my office.

" 'I'm in trouble,' she said.

"Suddenly the phone rang.

" 'This time we mean business.' the voice on the other end barked. 'Lay off or I'll send over a couple of my boys.'

"The line in my hand went dead.

"When I looked up, she had disappeared. But that's the way it goes in this business. Win a few, lose a few. The case was closed.

"Somewhere, outside, a dog was barking."

Looking back on it all, Elfman said the idea for his winning entry came to him out of the blue. Cliches from all corners of the country were flooding the offices of the Workman Publishing Co. in New York.

"I was a mere lad, just a face in the crowd," Elfman said. "But I hoped against hope. I gave it my best shot. That's really all any man can do."

For Elfman, it was "the thrill of a lifetime" when he ripped open the letter announcing his triumph. His beaming parents were proud as peacocks, but Elfman himself took it all in stride.

"Fame is fleeting," Elfman said. "I'm not going to rest on my laurels. I'm going to keep my shoulder to the wheel and my nose to the grindstone."

Elfman's ultimate goal is a career as a filmmaker. He and a friend produced one movie when Elfman was attending Westchester High School. It was called "Attack of the Killer Peanuts."

"We lost $80 on it," Elfman said. "But there are many pitfalls on the road to success. It's a long, hard journey to the top, and it's lonely when you get there. But I guess there's something inside me that just keeps driving me on."

Elfman's busy as a beaver these days, preparing for his trip to Miami Beach, pursuing his studies in cinema at UCLA and working weekends as a stock clerk at Fedco.

"I've always said a little hard work never hurt anybody," he said "If a job's worth doing, it's worth doing right."

Nonetheless, his heart is set on "getting away from it all" once he has his bags packed and is actually on his way to Miami Beach. Not only will he be lounging in luxury on the beach, he'll also be wined and dined at such fabled nightspots as the Club Gigi and the Boom Boom Room.

"I haven't decided who to take with me yet," Elfman said. "All my friends have been acting real friendly since I won. You know what they say: With friends like that, who needs enemies?"

Outside Elfman's apartment, gray clouds scuttled across the sky. Occasionally, the din of the rush-hour traffic wafted up through the open windows.

The atmosphere inside was warm and friendly. There was a temptation to linger, but my nose for news told me it was time to go.

"Miami Beach is a nice place to visit, but I wouldn't want to live there," Elfman said as I headed for the door.

"Yeah," I mumbled.

The door shut behind me. But that's the way it goes in this business. Win a few, lose a few. The interview was over.

Somewhere, outside, a dog was barking.[2]

---

[2]William Overend, "His Heart's in the Trite Place," *Los Angeles Times*, 25 October 1976. Copyright, 1976, Los Angeles Times, Reprinted by permission.

Cliches can be used to your advantage if you can turn around an expected word usage. "She's the worm in his apple," for instance, or "It's all sewage under the bridge."

Quotations. Most articles need quotations, and learning how to use quotation marks can be confusing.

1. Quoting a person in an article highlights words, so the words you quote should be important, Do not quote "I was born in Dallas, Texas." Save your quotes for interesting revelations ("I teach tennis, but I've never played the game") or controversial statements ("Medicare just isn't working. What about people who are too sick to pick up their food stamps?"). Be selective.

2. Most magazines use a journalistic style of attribution for material used from a publication, which is "According to _author_ in _title_," instead of including all publication information, such as place of publication, date, and publisher.

3. Whenever possible, keep quoted material together and do not break up sentences. However, quotations can appear several ways:

Partial quotation: He said she was a "gifted genius."

Interrupted quotation: "She was," he said, "a gifted genius."

Introductory attribution (which means the person quoted is listed at the beginning): He said, "She was a gifted genius."

Dangling attribution (which means the person quoted is listed at the end): "She was a gifted genius," he said.

4. When you carry a conversation from one paragraph to another, and the same person is talking, do not use quotation marks at the end of the first paragraph. Use them at the beginning of the second paragraph and all subsequent paragraphs until the speaker finishes, and then close the quotations.

5. In dialogue, begin and end a paragraph with quotation marks each time a new person speaks.

6. Do not use quotation marks to denote a euphemism, such as "passed away" or "rest room," or for current teenage jargon, such as "uptight" or "awesome."

7. Current style is to put all quotation marks outside of commas and periods.

"He was a pretty nice guy," she said.
"He was a pretty nice guy."
She said he was "nice," but not "pretty."

SMALL COMMON PROBLEMS

Active vs. passive verbs. Avoid "to be" verbs as much as possible and replace them with active verbs. "She was elected president by the committee" can be changed to "The committee elected her president."

Put statements in the positive. You will save words by saying "He was usually healthy" instead of "He was not very often sick."

Platitudes. This truism bores equally as much as the cliche. "All brides look beautiful on their wedding day" is an example.

Euphemisms. Avoid using words to replace uncomfortable words—"passed away" for *dead* or "slightly indisposed" for *drunk.*

Wordiness. That, which, and *what* are words (which) you can usually remove freely without changing your meaning. Also question every "there is" and "there are" and ask if you can reorganize the sentence. "There is a house on the hill" can become "A house is on the hill," for example.

YOUR FINAL DRAFT

When your article is ready for print, find the twenty-pound bond paper and begin. Make a carbon copy. Leave one-inch margins on all sides (see sample marked Your Title for format).

Name

Address

City, State, Zip

Phone

YOUR TITLE

by Your Name

The first page of your manuscript should look like this. Your margins should be one inch all around to allow room for editing marks. The first line (Name and Page) is typed six lines down from the top. Then go down ten spaces after the Phone and Social Security Number line and center your title in capitals. Go down two more spaces for "by" and your name. Four spaces down after that you can begin your manuscript.

Your manuscript should always be double-spaced, and you should indent for paragraphs. At the top of the second page, type your name at the left-hand margin, six spaces from the top, with a short description of your article. Type the page number at the right-hand margin. When you finish your article, put a mark (###) below the last paragraph to let your editor know you are finished.

Begin the second page six spaces from the top. Type your name, a dash, and a two-to three-word description of your topic (called a "slug") on the left-hand side (Example: Biagi—Catching Guppies) and on the right-hand side put the page number (Page 2 of 15). Then go down four spaces and begin typing. When you finish your article, put a mark (###) to indicate the end.

Corrections on your finished manuscript should be made with understandable editing marks. Use the marks sparingly, however, and retype any page with more than three corrections (see Editing Marks).

EDITING MARKS

The phone rang. Could it be that it was he? She sniffled into her pink linen handkerchief. Only yesterday he had been by side her. Now he was gone, gone forever.

The phone rang again. yesterday he had said it would never work, That a poor newspaper reporter from Peoria, Illinois, could never marry a rich newspaper publisher from Schenectady, New York. How wood he face his friends? How could he face his wife?

The phone rang again. She moved toward the antique pedestal table, which held the library's white princess telephone, Yes St. Laurent gown blowing past the Afghan hound Truffles, lying near the couch. Outside it was raining.

The phone rang again. Hello, she said desperately. Could it be her well-intentioned friend, Binky, or was it he?

paragraph
omit
transpose
omit a letter
capital
lower case
join
misspelling
separate
period
apostrophe
insert a word
comma
leave in
quotation marks
hyphen

MAILING THE MANUSCRIPT

You are now ready to mail the manuscript. A three-page article can be mailed folded in a rectangular number 10 envelope; an article any larger should be mailed in a manila envelope between two pieces of cardboard. If you have pictures to mail, check Chapter Nine for instructions on how to mail photographs with your manuscript. Paper clip, do not staple, your manuscript.

Manuscripts should be mailed first class. If you worry a lot, you can mail your manuscript certified with a return address card, which notifies you when the magazine received the article. The extra cost is minimal.

How long do you wait for a reply? A month is common, and six weeks is not unusual. At the end of six weeks, write a reminder note, mentioning the title of your article.

Magazines that pay on acceptance usually send you a note first accepting your article, with a general reference about the check being sent soon. Write a note acknowledging their acceptance and ask for three copies of the magazine in which your article appears. (You will have to buy the other forty-seven copies yourself.)

If the magazine pays on publication, write the same note asking for copies and add a line asking them to notify you when the article appears. A month to six weeks is a normal waiting time for your check, either after publication or after acceptance. After this, reminder notes help.

So, on to your next article (but check the Appendix for some hints about taxes and the names of writers' organizations). And remember Arnold Gingrich, *Esquire's* beloved editor, who said, "Writing, if seldom fun, is surprisingly often profitable."

A

Appendix :
The Writer
and Federal Taxes

*T*he money you make from writing is taxable income, but you will be happy to learn that you can deduct your writing expenses from that income.

First, the disclaimer. I am not an accountant, and any tax advice here does not reflect trained expertise. For accurate, current information on your tax status as a writer, consult your tax preparer or the Internal Revenue Service. Following is information that may help.

Travel and food. Keep a written record of cab or bus fares or parking fees and tolls with the date, destination, and cost. A pocket mileage record book (the cost of which is a writing expense) works well for this purpose. If you use a car, note mileage for writing-related travel. This can include trips to the post office, as well as travel to interviews and to the library. Also keep any hotel and plane ticket or train fare receipts, and receipts for any meals you buy for contacts or interviewees.

Writing supplies. Keep all receipts for a newly purchased typewriter or desk, desk chair, ribbons, typewriter table, filing cabinet, postage, pencils, pens, paper, erasers, scotch tape, books for research, or anything else you use for writing. Buy a ledger to note these expenses (the ledger is a writing expense).

Photography supplies. Keep receipts if you buy a camera, lenses, film, developing supplies, or camera case. Processing fees should also be noted.

Maintenance. Any repairs to your typewriter or camera (if you are a photographer) should be itemized. Also, if you have a maintenance contract for your typewriter, file your copy.

Communication. Record separately any charges for long-distance telephone calls you make for your writing. Also, save the receipts if you buy a tape recorder or cassettes and for photocopying costs.

Memberships. Keep a record of membership fees for writers' organizations, both national and local (see Appendix B for a listing).

Education. If you return to school to improve your writing skills, keep all records of enrollment and costs for books and transportation.

Also, file all correspondence—acceptances and rejections included—that will identify you as a working writer. Copies of your published articles are, of course, wonderful proof that you're working.

B

Appendix: Magazine Writers' Organizations

Writers' organizations are a helpful way to meet and share marketing information and contacts with writers in your special interest areas. Many writers' organizations also sponsor seminars where editors are invited to discuss their needs. Newsletters from many of these organizations are a valuable added membership benefit.

American Medical Writers Association, 5272 River Road, Suite 290, Bethesda, Maryland 20016

American Society of Journalists and Authors, Inc., 1501 Broadway, Suite 1907, New York, New York 10036.

Association of Petroleum Writers, 8824 E. 37 Place, Tulsa, Oklahoma 74145

Aviation/Space Writers Association, Cliffwood Road, Chester, New Jersey 07930

Construction Writers Association, 601 13 Street, N. W., Room 202, Washington, D. C. 20005

Dog Writers' Association of America, Kinney Hill Road, Washington Depot, Connecticut 06794

Education Writers Association, Box 281, Woodstown, New Jersey 08098

Garden Writers Association of America, 230 Park Avenue, New York, New York 10017

Golf Writers Association of America, 1720 Section Road, Suite 210, Cincinnati, Ohio 45237

International Association of Business Communicators, 870 Market Street, Suite 928, San Francisco, California 94102

National Association of Science Writers, Inc., Box 294, Greenlawn, New York 11740

National League of American Pen Women, Inc., 1300 17th Street, N. W., Washington, D. C. 20036

National Turf Writers Association, 6000 Executive Boulevard, Suite 317, Rockville, Maryland 20852

National Writers Club, 1450 S. Havana, Suite 620, Aurora, Colorado 80012

Outdoor Writers Association of America, 4141 W. Bradley Road, Milwaukee, Wisconsin 53209

P.E.N.-American Center, 47 Fifth Avenue, New York, New York 10003

Society of American Travel Writers, 1120 Connecticut Avenue, N. W., Suite 940, Washington, D. C. 20036

United States Ski Writers Association, 7 Kensington Road, Glens Falls, New York 12801

United States Tennis Writers Association, 156 Broad Street, Lynn, Massachusetts 01901

Washington Independent Writers Association, National Press Building, Suite 13, Terrace Level, Washington, D. C. 20045

Western Writers of America, Inc., Route 1, Box 35H, Victor, Montana 59875

Women in Communications, Inc., Box 9561, Austin, Texas 78766

Index